Team-Based Professional Development

A Process for School Reform

Judith T. Witmer
Steven A. Melnick

ROWMAN & LITTLEFIELD EDUCATION
Lanham, Marland • *Toronto* • *Plymouth, UK*
2007

Published in the United States of America
by Rowman & Littlefield Education
A Division of Rowman & Littlefield Publishers, Inc.
A wholly owned subsidiary of The Rowman & Littlefield Publishing Group, Inc.
4501 Forbes Boulevard, Suite 200, Lanham, Maryland 20706
www.rowmaneducation.com

Estover Road
Plymouth PL6 7PY
United Kingdom

British Library Cataloguing in Publication Information Available

Library of Congress Cataloging-in-Publication Data

Witmer, Judith T.
   Team-based professional development : a process for school reform / Judith T. Witmer, Steven A. Melnick.
      p. cm.
   Includes bibliographical references.
   ISBN-13: 978-1-57886-536-9 (hardcover : alk. paper)
   ISBN-10: 1-57886-536-0 (hardcover : alk. paper)
   ISBN-13: 978-1-57886-537-6 (pbk. : alk. paper)
   ISBN-10: 1-57886-537-9 (pbk. : alk. paper)
   1. Teachers—Training of—United States. 2. Team learning approach in education—United States. 3. Educational change—United States. I. Melnick, Steven A. II. Title.
LB1715.M375 2007
370.17'5—dc22

2006023261

♾️™ The paper used in this publication meets the minimum requirements of American National Standard for Information Sciences—Permanence of Paper for Printed Library Materials, ANSI/NISO Z39.48-1992.
Manufactured in the United States of America.

Contents

Foreword *Vince Rizzo*   v

Acknowledgments   ix

1   What If? The Case for Team-Based Professional Development—A New Model for Professional Growth   1

2   How Did We Get Here? Design Options for a Professional Development Continuum   12

3   Teachers Who Asked *What If?* Criteria for Successful Team-Based Professional Development   23

4   Can You Do This? Successful Programs   37

5   Taking One Step at a Time: Initiating and Implementing Team-Based Professional Development   58

6   How Do You Know It's Working? Organizing and Monitoring Professional Development Programs   82

7   What If It Happens? Institutionalizing and Sustaining Team-Based Professional Development   96

References   117

Foreword

Pluralitas non est ponenda sine neccesitate: Plurality should not be posited without necessity.

—Occam's razor

What if school reform emanates from a simple, logical, and inexpensive process that is easy to identify and implement? And what if this process is readily available to all school districts without the need for wholesale changes to the program?

The answers to these thought-provoking questions form the core of Judith Witmer and Steven Melnick's study of team-based professional development. Having had the pleasure to participate in the Keystone Integrated Framework Project, I was witness to the power of the team-based model designed by these two authors and described in this book. To borrow a phrase, its beauty is in the details.

For years, educators have searched for the holy grail of school reform, asking "What changes really matter?" Witmer and Melnick have discovered the locus of reform hidden deep within the education's richest and most plentiful resource: its practitioners.

The concept is too obvious, too transparent for today's overly complex and analytical times. That the capital needed to transform educational practice exists within an ongoing plan to organize teacher development and training may boggle some minds. Yet, as defined by

Occam's razor, the simplicity and elegance of Witmer and Melnick's concept gives it its power. In truth, school districts have on staff the experts needed for authentic and meaningful reform. Further, the nation's schools have within their ranks the source of their continual improvement—a purpose beyond reform.

In this age in which the teaching profession is dismissed or maligned as being part of the problem, the authors suggest the very opposite. Their argument is that a thoughtful revision of the current practice of professional development—from its current, didactic formula to a team-based model—is regenerative for teachers, schools, districts, and education in general. In effect, the process becomes the reform. What their team-based model recognizes—and what the current development models ignore—is that focusing educational professionals on continual improvement, program excellence, and problem solving pierces the veil spun by critics that shrouds the reputation of public schools. These critics smugly suggest revision and reform from their perches outside the fray, often to fit their own narrow purposes. Politicians and for-profit corporate sales staffs, as modern-day mountebanks, sell their versions of reform as an elixir. They expect that educators should invite their critics to solve the complex problems facing their profession. Would any other profession relinquish control of its destiny? By asking teachers and administrators to work together in a cooperative sustaining venture, Witmer and Melnick give educators the tools to reshape their destiny.

Team-based professional development is metacognitive; it allows educators to reflect on their practice, and it helps their practice evolve. It places educators in control of their profession by asking them to marshal their knowledge and creativity in their chosen domain. The power of this simple process can be clearly noted in the words of educators who practiced it as part of their association with the Keystone project. Clearly, they have been transformed by their experience. As you read their responses to a recent survey about their Keystone project experiences 10 years past, you will see that, once learned, the process becomes ingrained in one's practice. For those who can initiate it, team-based professional development can continue as part of one's planning and implementing new standards for classroom practice. For those who are no longer able to sustain the practice, they are cursed with the knowledge of an untapped resource.

This book is for all education professionals. As a school improvement tool, Witmer and Melnick's vision helps teachers and administrators manage change and growth. As a process for reform, it is an important consideration for current practitioners and those who prepare teacher candidates in colleges and universities. Given the argument's clarity, one is left with the real question left unanswered: *Why not?*

Vince Rizzo
Director of the Howard Gardner School for Discovery,
Scranton, PA

Acknowledgments

First, thanks to Beth Cornell, fine arts and humanities advisor, Pennsylvania Department of Education, who had the original idea for the Keystone Integrated Framework Project, a federally funded program promoting the integration of the arts with civics, English, geography, and history. It was Beth's creative vision that teachers, administrators, and higher education faculty could work together as a local team, developing curriculum, preparing the teachers to teach integrated lessons, and encouraging teacher preparation programs to include instruction in the process of curriculum integration. We served as director and evaluator for the project and soon realized that we were attracted to the Keystone project because of the team-based concept, work, and research that we had conducted independently.

We are most grateful to the Keystone project teams and their commitment to team-based professional development, which was an idea familiar to a few, one totally new to others, and one challenging to all. In particular, we wish to acknowledge the sustained success of Mountain View High School, a site that continues with its humanities elective that was developed for the project; we treasure its continuing commitment and the friendships that we formed with George Barbolish, Peter Regeski, and Madonna Munley. We also salute Vince Rizzo, a visionary in his own right, then curriculum director for Scranton City School District who, along with Beth Burkhauser, art teacher, made it happen for McNichols Plaza Elementary School.

Other leaders included Barbara Pominek, then coordinator of curriculum and instruction, and Deborah Sasala, elementary music teacher, of Indiana School District, as well as Dr. Leigh Altadonna, assistant superintendent, Abington School District. Also, we salute Donna Baker, Conneaut Valley High School, for her determination to deliver the best to her students despite insurmountable odds.

1

What If? The Case for Team-Based Professional Development—A New Model for Professional Growth

What if teachers came to school the way the best students do? What if they were eager to see their colleagues, excited about discussing what is important in the classes that they are teaching that day? What if they all were energized to make plans and were ready to take on the day? What if teachers worked in real teams, with a common planning period during which they planned the schedule, work, and activities for the day, the week, or even the year? What if teachers in a particular team shared the same students, getting to know them from the point of view of each individual teacher? What if teachers were able to meet with parents from a common approach, a shared knowledge of each student's progress, and a joint plan for that student's improvement? And what if the teachers felt ownership of their day and the students whom they shared with team members? What if, for the first time, they felt vested and enfranchised? And what if this could happen at your school?

If you are tired of professional development days that direct you to "attend this in-service" or "study this program" or "go to this county institute"; if you resent being herded here and commandeered there in the stereotypically paternalistic style of a school district; and, most important, if you are weary of obediently following orders and seeing no results, then you need to know that there is a better way to approach your continuing education and organize the teaching and learning process. Further, if you are concerned that what you usually learn in these professional development sessions might work for your own class but still leave you isolated in your own classroom, never knowing how your course plays a part in your students' overall education, it is time to take stock.

In general, teaching is one of the loneliest professions, with limited opportunities to work with colleagues toward a common goal. It does not have to be this way. Isn't it time to stop habitually repetitious and unsuccessful practices and consider a process and a model that first look at what it is that teachers value and what it is that teachers believe most helps them in their day-to-day delivery of instruction? Isn't it time to find creative ways to include research-based practices in your teaching? Isn't it time to look at a model that is supported by research focused on the area of professionalism? And isn't it time to take a good look at the possibilities offered through team-based professional development, a process that can transform you and your colleagues into a vibrant unit on a common mission: students who achieve.

Studies support this relationship between professional learning communities and improved student achievement. As Hudis, Calderon, and Sanborn (2005) reported, "a study by WestEd (2000) found that in eight award-winning public schools, professional development programs were characterized by collaborative structures, diverse and extensive professional learning opportunities, and an emphasis on accountability and student results" (p. 10). A study of 11,000 students enrolled in 820 secondary schools (Lee, Smith, & Croninger, 1995) found that in schools with learning communities, students achieved larger academic gains in mathematics, science, history, and reading than students did in traditionally organized schools. In addition, a longitudinal study by McLaughlin and Talbert (1993) reported how 16 high schools in California and Michigan used professional communities as a strategy for student intervention and teacher reform. And when examining characteristics of schools that successfully connected restructuring initiatives to improved student learning, Newmann and Wehlage (1995) observed that these schools "functioned as professional learning communities" (pp. 10–11).

These successes provide concern for those advocating reform, including measures such as team-based professional development—namely, their concern is that traditional professional development has not been successful, because it has not led to positive changes in the way that teachers teach and students learn. As noted by Kelly (1999), traditional professional development is "widely evidenced by the lack of change in teacher behaviors," and, unfortunately, school administrators continue "to dictate conventional in-service programs for practicing teachers" (p. 427). Further, Kelly made an excellent observation that traditional in-service programming focuses on perceived teacher weaknesses; thus, the whole process begins with negative overtones. This observation supports an earlier comment by C. M. Clark (1995): that teachers typically do not relish being humiliated as a prerequisite to learning and development. In the experience of most teachers, this predisposition has not changed.

Although much research has been published detailing the impact of various new approaches to professional development (e.g., Bos, Mather, Narr, & Babur, 1999; Bruckerhoff & Bruckerhoff, 1997; Fullan, 1991; Glatthorn, 1990; Shroyer, Ramey-Gassert, Hancock, Moore, & Walker, 1995; Voltz, 1995), they have not had much impact on actual practice. Even with changes improving the impact in classrooms of professional development through teacher induction programs, peer coaching, and professional development schools, the results have not had sufficient breadth or depth to cause systemic positive change in the districts using them. Recent research has supported these findings (Hudis et al., 2005) and, more important, has suggested that what may be missing is that the approach to professional development for teachers continues to be imposed onto them and delivered into them. This research calls for viewing teachers in a way different from that which students are viewed in a classroom—and, typically, that which teacher professional development has been viewed—because teachers are not children. Professional development should have its basis in adult learning theory because teachers are, first and foremost, adults (Merriam, 2001). Team-based professional development is grounded in the premise that teachers are adults and that their continuing education programs should be adult centered.

ADULT LEARNING

It is alarming to realize that adult learning theory is rarely considered or applied in designing professional development for teachers. Professional development has been structured in the same way that lessons are developed for children, even though evidence indicates that adults do not learn the way that children learn. Thus, it seems reasonable that if one is planning education for adults, one needs to understand how adults learn, and one needs to plan teacher professional development according to its theories.

Of the many adult learning models, all can be traced to three primary schools of thought, all pertinent to the team-based professional development model: self-directed learning; transformational learning; and andragogy, "the art and science of helping adults learn" (Merriam & Caffarella, 1999, p. 272).

Self-Directed Learning

Self-directed learning may seem self-evident, but it is worth examining, because it is foundational to the emphasis that higher education places on developing lifelong self-directed learners. Although one might wonder why this emphasis has not affected schools in planning their professional development, the fact that higher education deems self-directed learning a necessary element to the sustainability of any adult program is reason to understand its three primary goals:

1. To enhance the ability of adult learners to be self-directed
2. To foster transformational learning
3. To promote emancipatory learning and social action

The first goal suggests that personal growth is a primary objective of self-directed learning. Brockett and Hiemstra (1991) stated that "individuals possess virtually unlimited potential for growth . . . [and] that only by accepting responsibility for one's own learning is it possible to take a proactive approach to the learning process" (pp. 26–27). The majority of process models in self-directed learning focus on this first goal.

The second goal suggests that learners must reflect critically while having an understanding of "the historical, cultural, and biographical reasons for one's needs, wants, and interests. . . . Such self-knowledge is a prerequisite for autonomy in self-directed learning" (Mezirow, 1985, p. 27). To reflect critically, learners must accept responsibility for their own learning and be proactive, as consistently noted by Linda Darling-Hammond (1996), a nationally recognized expert on professional development. According to Merriam and Caffarella (1999), this goal is grounded in the theories of Maslow (1970) and Rogers (1969, 1983).

Proponents of the third goal believe that adults must examine the sociopolitical assumptions under which they learn and function and that the process must include collective action as an outcome of adult learning (Merriam & Caffarella, 1999). In short, adult learners must exert control over their own learning and, equally important, what they do with their newfound knowledge. Brookfield (1993) suggested what should be a consistent element of self-directed learning—that learners exercise control over all educational decisions. As important as the researchers in adult learning find these goals, such goals are largely, and unfortunately, ignored in district-planned professional development for teachers.

Grow's staged self-directed learning model (1991), in particular, has relevance for teachers and professional development, because teachers' attitudes, knowledge, and skills vary widely on any given topic. Grow suggested that there are four aspects of self-directed learning that frame knowledge in a way that professional development planners find useful:

1. Learners of low self-direction need an authority figure.
2. Learners of moderate self-direction are motivated and confident but largely ignorant of the subject matter.
3. Learners of intermediate self-direction have both the skill and the basic knowledge, and they view themselves as ready and able to explore with a good guide.
4. Learners of high self-direction are willing and able to plan, execute, and evaluate their own learning with or without the help of an expert.

In light of these findings, it is strongly advisable to plan professional development processes that move teachers who are not self-directed to a level of self-directed learning. A team-based process provides this opportunity.

Transformational Learning

Based on the early work of Mezirow (1978), transformational learning focuses more on the cognitive process than do either self-directed learning or andragogy. It concentrates on "mental construction of experience, inner meaning, and reflection" (Merriam & Caffarella, 1999, p. 318). As Clark (1993) stated, "transformational learning *shapes* people;

they are different afterward in ways both they and others can recognize" (p. 47).

Transformational learning involves three processes: critical reflection on one's own assumptions, discussion to validate the reflective insight, and action (Merriam & Caffarella, 1999; Mezirow, 1978). The transformational learning process of questioning assumptions, biases, beliefs, and values allows new understandings to emerge that, in turn, guide future decisions. The focus on critical reflection, discussion, and action (functions of an adult) is an important component of effective professional development and is critical to team-based professional development.

Andragogy

Knowles (1968) proposed a model of adult learning that he labeled *andragogy*, which attempts to distinguish itself from preadult schooling. His later work (Knowles, 1984) refined this model, which he based on the following four assumptions about the design of learning experiences for adults: First, adults need to know why they need to learn something. Second, effective adult learning is experiential—that is, derived from experience rather than inference. Third, adults' approach to learning focuses on problem solving. Fourth, adults learn best when they see immediate value to the topic. (A fifth factor has sometimes been added by others, which suggests that adults are motivated to learn by internal factors rather than external factors.)

Knowles (1984) also identified some important characteristics of adult learners:

- Adults are autonomous and self-directed.
- Adults have accumulated a broad foundation of life experiences and knowledge.
- Adults are goal oriented.
- Adults are relevancy oriented.
- Adults are practical, focusing on what is most useful to them in their work.
- Adults, like all learners, need to be shown respect.

Each of the three primary viewpoints in adult learning contributes to and has application for professional development for teachers, particularly for team-based professional development. In particular, Knowles's characteristics of adult learners (1984) underscore the differences between lessons for children and professional development activities for teachers.

Although self-directed learning is said to foster lifelong learning, studies on self-directed learning are still emerging. However, the four levels of self-directed learning presented by Grow's staged self-directed learning model (1991) are particularly relevant in planning professional development activities. Taking into account that the level of self-directedness of adult learners has an impact on the success of any professional development effort, it is important that those responsible for professional development initiatives pay close attention to adult learning theory.

Although self-directed learning and andragogy are necessary to formulating a plan for professional development, transformational learning appears to be the most relevant. The elements of transformational learning—critical reflection, discourse (discussion), and action—are the essence of professional development and embody the very activities important to sustained systemic change.

More recently, research has called for a focus on incorporating adult learning theory into educational programs for adults. In particular, those who teach adults at the university level and provide ongoing professional development for teachers are being encouraged to include elements of transformative learning in their interactions with adults (e.g., Cranton & King, 2003; King, 2002; Lawler & King, 2003; Taylor, 1997). Some of that research has focused on professional development for teachers. Cranton and King (2003) observed that professional development activities, when they are available, tend to be seen as not valuable, perhaps because they are not grounded in adult learning theory. In our examination of past professional development efforts for teachers (see Melnick & Schubert, 1997; Melnick & Witmer, 1999; Witmer & Melnick, 1997), it is clear that the reflection, discourse, and action so essential to transformational learning are typically not a substantive part of teachers' professional development experiences but are such an important component in team-based professional development. The importance of such a framework is underscored by Cranton and King (2003):

> Transformative learning takes place when this process leads us to open up our frame of reference, discard a habit of mind, see alternatives, and thereby act differently in the world (Mezirow and Associates, 2000).

When educators are led to examine their practice critically and thereby acquire alternative ways of understanding what they do, transformative learning about teaching takes place (Cranton, 1996). It seems that this must be a goal of professional development. If we do not consciously think about and reflect on our practice, we become nothing more than automatons following a dubious set of rules or principles—rules or principles that are unlikely to be relevant in the ever-changing, complex context of teaching and learning. (p. 32)

Given these assumptions and the characteristics of professional development for teachers, it is clear that most current professional development programs are not consistent with what is known about adult learning theory and are therefore not likely to be successful. What professional development planners can learn from adult learning theory is that activities must involve adults as active participants rather than passive recipients. In short, the content of professional development should emerge from teachers themselves, because they have a better understanding of what they need and are more likely to participate in activities that they deem important.

Using transformational learning as a foundation, King (2002) examined professional development for teachers in the use of technology. King concluded that, rather than simply focus on teaching specific skills, as has been done in the past, professional development should instead incorporate group discussions, collaborative work groups, and curriculum development to help teachers rethink their concepts of teaching and learning. By using what the literature says about learners, King postulated that professional developers can create active learning environments that include collaborative experiences and result in effective learning experiences for teachers.

The revised standards of the National Staff Development Council (2001) reflect the importance of key components of adult learning theory. The 12 standards are organized around context, process, and content. The context standards focus on the creation of learning communities, effective leadership, and appropriate resources. The process standards bring attention to applying research, the use of data-driven decision making, the importance of systematic evaluation, and the appropriate design of activities to incorporate what is known about learning theory. In addition, the process standards call for teachers to have the requisite knowledge and skills to foster collaboration. Finally, the content standards emphasize the importance of equity, quality teaching, and family involvement. All 12 standards are clearly important in fostering effective professional development. It seems logical that ensuring the necessary context—that is, one including learning communities, leadership, and resources—is a first step in developing the processes and content necessary to effect systemic change.

Focusing first on building a community of learners with effective leadership and sufficient resources creates an environment where teachers take control of their learning. Although many studies have been done on collaborative professional development (e.g., Bos et al., 1999; Calderon, 1995; Cleland et al., 1999; Glatthorn, 1990; Shroyer et al., 1995), they have addressed only one National Staff Development Council standard (learning communities) and, for the most part, have not addressed other standards in process and content. Although collaborative professional development leads to teacher involvement and includes the reflection, discourse, and action of transformative learning, without a framework that includes the National Staff Development Council standards of context, process, and content, little systemic change is likely to occur.

Adult learning theory should provide the basis for experiences and activities aimed at professional development for teachers. Once it is established that this professional development is adult centered, the next consideration is the organizational structure of schools. To lessen the isolation of individual teachers and to develop a school community approach to the young citizens (the students), teachers working together to improve teaching and learning makes sense. Not only is this approach efficient, but, more important, a collaborative structure to professional development contributes to an overall sense of purpose and a community of learners. With these vital elements, the collaborative structure suggests the seeds for rich team-based professional development that has its roots in collaboration but goes beyond its basic premises.

TEAM-BASED PROFESSIONAL DEVELOPMENT

One can interpret *team based* in many ways, but the term *team-based professional development* describes a model in which small teams of teachers with common interests help one another learn about their own learning; study and reflect on their own teaching; develop ongoing, sustained professional relationships with each other; and take responsibility for their own professional growth and development. Ideally, members of the small teams share the same students.

The ideas behind team-based professional development are not new but are based on the research of those whose findings show that teachers need to become actively involved in and take responsibility for their own professional development. According to Darling-Hammond (1996), "professional development needs to foster teacher professionalism through networking, inquiry, and reflection with more effective, problem-based approaches that are built into teachers' on-going work with colleagues" (p. 10). She continued by saying that teachers who are actively involved in their own professional development—who have access to teacher networks, enriched professional roles, and collegial work—feel positive about staying in the profession. This view is supported by earlier research that found that when teachers feel like true professionals and are treated as such, they become committed to the profession and are effective in the classroom (Haggstrom, Darling-Hammond, & Grissmer, 1988; McLaughlin & Talbert, 1993; Rosenholtz, 1989). Sykes (1996) added that teachers must engage in learning about their own learning, in studying about their own teaching, and in sustaining relationships with other teachers. To reform education, teachers, rather than policymakers, must play an active role to improve teaching and learning, particularly their own. By taking an active role through team-based professional development processes, teachers can move the profession toward systemic reform.

From a statewide curriculum integration project involving 11 school districts across Pennsylvania, Melnick and Schubert (1997) identified a set of factors that, when in place, enhance a school's chances of success in the project. Utilizing a qualitative, multisite, modified analytic induction design, the researchers examined factors identified in research literature that delineate the roles of teachers and administrators in school reform (e.g., Peters, Schubeck, & Hopkins, 1995; Wepner, 1993a, 1993b; Williams & Reynolds, 1993), as well as those that foster a successful organizational climate (e.g., Fullan, 1991; Osborne, 1993a, 1993b). Factors such as provision of adequate resources (e.g., time to work together), teacher teaming, organizational support, and communication were thought to be important and were present in the five most successful sites. The remaining six sites lacked one or more areas.

Using previous research (Melnick & Schubert, 1997; Witmer & Melnick, 1997) regarding the effectiveness of this type of professional development, we (Melnick & Witmer, 1999) further investigated the perceptions of teachers regarding their own professional development along five distinct constructs—teaming, time, organizational support, communication, and professional responsibility—and compared the perceptions of teachers who utilized these constructs in professional development with the perceptions of their colleagues who did not. Teachers involved in team-based professional development activities had significantly higher perceptions of their own professional development. What is most promising—and exciting—about the team-based professional development model is that, like its premise, it evolved from the teachers themselves, yet its characteristics are supported by research. This book describes the model and, through the use of examples in schools where it emerged, discusses its implementation and provides a recipe for success for team-based professional development.

2

How Did We Get Here? Design Options for a Professional Development Continuum

In the summer of 1924, Miss Jessie Pifer attended her first summer class at Clarion Normal School in central Pennsylvania, where she eventually spent the next three summers preparing to be certified as a schoolteacher. Jessie and her fellow first-year students found themselves taking basic courses such as English Fundamentals, Health I, Primary Methods, and School Efficiency. True to the prevailing attitude of the time that the equivalent of only 1 year of teaching methods was needed to teach elementary school—because teaching children was simple!—Jessie was fully confident that she could teach all grades in an elementary school because she had already attended 12 years of public school. Her classmates agreed, "What can be so difficult teaching material we already know?"

At the end of the first summer's session, Miss Pifer was issued a partial certificate, making her eligible to teach "in Clearfield County until August 1, 1925, the subjects prescribed for the curriculum of the elementary school." This certificate received an official annual renewal through August 1928, at which time its holder would presumably be granted permanent certification. Because the state school system was governed through the counties, all teachers desiring school positions were registered with the counties in which they resided or had filed an intent. The hiring process usually included an interview with a five-member local or township board, and employment was referred to as "being given a school." Jessie was 19 years old when she began her first year of teaching in a one-room school 3 miles from her home.

In the original county system, schools typically closed for 2 weeks at Christmastime, beginning around December 20, at which time the teachers were expected to attend Teachers' Institute, a 3-day series of meetings and lectures held from morning until late in the evening. However, by 1926, when Jessie was a 2-year veteran, the institute had been moved to the end of the summer over 5 days, from Monday afternoon, August 30, through Friday morning, September 3. Miss Pifer, an experienced teacher, found listening to the six addresses (none of which had titles) to be tiresome each day, as evidenced by her handwritten notes in the program.

Two years later, the Sixty-Fifth Annual Session of the Clearfield County Teachers' Institute was held on August 27–31, 1928, in the high school auditorium of Clearfield High School. This institute program cautioned all teachers wishing full credit to be enrolled by 1:30 p.m. on August 27. The institute fee of $3.50 (3% of a typical monthly salary and equivalent to today's teachers paying a $120 fee) included membership in the Pennsylvania State Education Association. A sampling of topic titles over the 5 days included "Science and the Future," "A Professional Attitude for the Teacher," and "Fighting the Good Fight." County certificates were awarded to eighth-grade students who had read and prepared a written report on 10 books. Also included in the program were sessions entitled "A Healthy Creed for Teachers" and "Beatitudes for the Teacher" and those that revolved around practical issues such as classroom lighting and ventilation and how to display the flag.

In Clearfield County, Pennsylvania, Teacher Institutes were created in the early 19th century, tracing its formal institutes to 1863 with a handful of rural teachers in attendance. By 1895 more than 400 teachers attended, and by 1926 the number had grown to 509. Although Guskey (1986) characterized early and subsequent professional development efforts as being disorganized and filled with controversy, such did not seem to be the case in Pennsylvania. There, the largest controversy in 1887 was whether to change the writing styles taught in the county schools from slanted to vertical. Other concerns included the question of whether high schools require enough U.S. history and whether novels should be part of a school library's collection.

By the last quarter of the 20th century, in-service education had generally become 1-day events planned by administrators, conducted by

outside experts, and presented to teachers, many of whom were passive recipients because they saw little relevance in what was being said
to what they were doing in their classrooms. Ernest Boyer (1983) did
his best to point out that it is unrealistic to expect teachers who were
trained 20 years earlier to prepare students to live 40 years into the future, without some relevant process of systematic continuing education.

BACKGROUND

Even at the present time, one of the most crucial yet often-forgotten
aspects of professional development involves just the point that Boyer
(1983) was making, reflected in the "so what?" attitude of many
teachers who believe that their time is being wasted. That crucial aspect of professional development is the absolute necessity for the involvement of teachers in (a) identifying possible solutions to instructional and programmatic problems that they are experiencing and (b)
developing a school climate conducive to change—change that the
teachers have identified as a need. Teachers' acknowledgment of this
need and their involvement in identifying ways to meet the need set
the stage for their ownership of professional development and led to
their active involvement in professional development activities.

Because of a growing consensus that professional development
must be at the center of instructional improvement (Elmore & Burney,
1997; Haslam & Seremet, 2001), improving teaching is finally becoming a cornerstone of the efforts to create better schools. Noted education researcher Harold Wenglinsky (2000) made the point that
"unless a child is taught by competent teachers, the impact of other
education reforms will be diminished" (p. 3). In short, students learn
more from good teachers than from poor teachers in any circumstance, so the primary charge is to try to make the poorer teachers better. However, because even good teachers cannot automatically take
the research findings and infuse them into how they deliver instruction, the process of professional development is needed to take the research findings and translate them into focused, long-term site-based
approaches. The point of this professional development is to target
specific classroom practices (Willis, 2002).

Recognition that professional development training requires more
than knowledge activities suggests the necessity for a multidimen-

sional approach to professional development. As a result, recent approaches have conceptualized professional development along three dimensions: knowledge, attitudes, and behaviors. If the intent of professional development is to acquire knowledge, then large-group presentations are efficient in terms of time and cost. However, such presentations are thought to be ineffective in effecting systemic change. On the other hand, if the focus of professional development centers more on changing attitudes and developing skills, a shift is necessary toward interactive, participatory models that engage teachers in their own professional development. Ideally, then, for a teacher to effectively utilize a new teaching technique, it is necessary for the teacher to have a knowledge of the technique, a positive attitude toward it, and the necessary skills to implement the technique successfully in the classroom. What has been learned, however, is that although these three dimensions—knowledge, attitude, skills— are necessary, they are not sufficient for systemic change. Such change can come about only with cooperative learning, collaboration, and teaming.

In the mid-1990s, the U.S. Department of Education's Professional Development Team (1995) identified 10 principles of effective teacher professional development. According to these principles, effective professional development does the following:

Focuses on teachers as central to student learning, yet includes all other members of the school community.

Focuses on individual, collegial, and organizational improvement.

Respects and nurtures the intellectual and leadership capacity of teachers, principals, and others in the school community.

Reflects best available research and practice in teaching, learning, and leadership.

Enables teachers to develop further expertise in subject content, teaching strategies, uses of technologies, and other essential elements in teaching to high standards.

Promotes continuous inquiry and improvement embedded in the daily life of schools.

Is planned collaboratively by those who will participate in and facilitate that development.

Requires substantial time and other resources.

Is driven by a coherent long-term plan.

Is evaluated ultimately on the basis of its impact on teacher effectiveness and student learning; and this assessment guides subsequent professional development efforts. (p. 6)

These principles have helped to lay the groundwork for rich models of professional development, models in which teachers become engaged in the overall conceptual approach to working as a team.

In 2001, the National Staff Development Council adopted revised standards for professional development that focus on context, process, and content (see Table 2.1). The council suggested that teachers be involved in learning communities, with the necessary administrative leadership and resources to effect change. Further, data-driven

Table 2.1.   National Staff Development Council Standards for Staff Development

Context standards
Staff development that improves the learning of all students:
   Organizes adults into learning communities whose goals are aligned with those of the school and district. (Learning communities)
   Requires skillful school and district leaders who guide continuous instructional improvement. (Leadership)
   Requires resources to support adult learning and collaboration. (Resources)

Process standards
Staff development that improves the learning of all students:
   Uses disaggregated student data to determine adult learning priorities, monitor progress, and help sustain continuous improvement. (Data driven)
   Uses multiple sources of information to guide improvement and demonstrate its impact. (Evaluation)
   Prepares educators to apply research to decision making. (Research based)
   Uses learning strategies appropriate to the intended goal. (Design)
   Applies knowledge about human learning and change. (Learning)
   Provides educators with the knowledge and skills to collaborate. (Collaboration)

Content standards
Staff development that improves the learning of all students:
   Prepares educators to understand and appreciate all students, create safe, orderly and supportive learning environments, and hold high expectations for their academic achievement. (Equity)
   Deepens educators' content knowledge, provides them with research-based instructional strategies to assist students in meeting rigorous academic standards, and prepares them to use various types of classroom assessments appropriately. (Quality teaching)
   Provides educators with knowledge and skills to involve families and other stakeholders appropriately. (Family involvement)

Note: National Staff Development Council (2001).

decision making, multiple sources of information, and research-based instructional decisions were deemed necessary to the process, as were effective professional development programs that provide teachers with the knowledge and skills to work and plan collaboratively. Finally, the council's standards call for teachers to hold high expectations for all students while providing a safe and orderly environment for learning. In sum, the National Staff Development Council laid the groundwork for professional development to enhance teachers' content knowledge, increase their use of research-based instructional strategies and assessments, and provide them with the knowledge and skills to involve families and other stakeholders appropriately. The council's work provided affirmation for those who had already been working in teams because it felt right and were willing to struggle with the process before it became formalized.

Placing professional development practices along a continuum of professional involvement provides a way to see the increase of teacher involvement as professional development practices move from 1-day programs to team-based professional development (Figure 2.1). It is

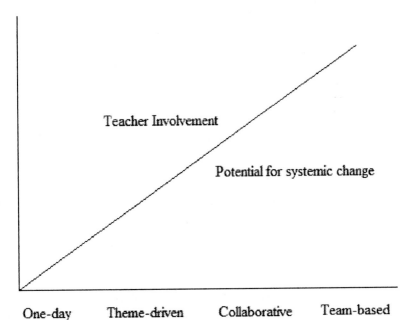

Teacher Involvement

Potential for systemic change

One-day   Theme-driven   Collaborative   Team-based

Figure 2.1.   Professional Development Contiuum

important to note that 1-day professional development programs offer little in the way of systemic change and that the implications are strong for substantive systemic change with increased teacher involvement.

SUMMARY OF DESIGN OPTIONS

One-Day Inservice Programs

One-day in-service programs typically focus on providing information to large groups of teachers. Districts using this approach center on broad goals of the district or school. Primarily effective for acquiring knowledge, this type of in-service program usually requires minimal planning and is often the least expensive professional development option available to school districts. As such, it is widely used.

Regrettably, teachers typically have little input into the planning process or even the content of such 1-day programs. These in-service days are often administratively planned with little teacher involvement and do not focus on changing attitudes and developing skills. Teachers are not organized into any type of learning communities or collaborative groups that sustain discussion, let alone effect any change. Due to the short-term nature of these days, little data-driven and research-based decision making come into play. Collaboration is rarely used. As can be seen in Figure 2.1, this type of professional development has low teacher involvement and rarely leads to any systemic change sustained over time.

Theme-Driven Professional Development

Theme-driven professional development activities increase the level of teacher involvement and, consequently, the potential for systemic change. Theme-driven professional development usually consists of multiday programs that are coordinated, interconnected, and intended to provide a range of training dimensions (i.e., knowledge, attitudes, skills). As many districts schedule three or more in-service days in the annual school calendar, theme-driven professional development days have the potential to make some meaningful changes to classroom instruction. These coordinated days may focus on specific program initiatives that are intended to improve instruction—for example, improving standardized test scores in reading. The content of these days is often standards driven.

Although there may be more teacher involvement in the planning of theme-driven days than what is apparent in 1-day professional development activities, these themed days are still predominantly planned and driven by the administration. "Experts" are brought in to work with teachers over an extended period of time. There is increased opportunity for collaboration among teachers, but it is not necessarily central to the activities provided. Unfortunately, when the theme-driven cycle concludes, little, if any, sustainable change has occurred, and teachers simply await the next wave of inevitable initiatives.

Collaborative Professional Development

Collaborative professional development provides an opportunity for the participants to establish learning communities. This type of professional development is teacher driven and more closely addresses some of the National Staff Development Council standards. Teachers using this model typically use data and research to make decisions about their teaching and about improving student achievement. Using a collaborative model, professional development activities are goal oriented and focused on developing the knowledge and skills necessary to positively affect student learning.

As discussed in chapter 1, many of these efforts result in single initiatives that focus on a specific problem. In some cases, when the problem is solved, the collaboration wanes. There is little evidence in the literature suggesting that such collaboration is sustained. Characteristically, additional resources and training are needed to provide teams of teachers with the knowledge and skills to continue collaborating.

Team-Based Professional Development

Team-based professional development is a model in which small teams of teachers with common interests help one another learn about their own learning; study and reflect on their own teaching; develop ongoing, sustained professional relationships with each other; and take responsibility for their own professional growth and development. Teachers are organized into small learning communities, and administrative involvement and support are imperative. Although team-based professional development does not require substantial resources, some resources (both human and financial) are required to support elements such as common planning time for team meetings and an occasional release day. Some training is required to help teams learn to work together in identifying their professional development needs, preparing action plans to achieve their goals, reflecting on their own progress, and evaluating the extent to which they have met their goals.

Based on previous research (Melnick & Schubert, 1997; Melnick & Witmer, 1999; Witmer & Melnick, 1997), a number of key factors need to be in place to enhance the likelihood of success: adequate resources (mainly, time to work together), teacher teaming, organizational support, and communication. When implemented fully, the model has the potential for high teacher involvement, effecting systemic change, changing the professional roles and lives of the teachers involved, and resulting in an increase in student achievement.

FACTORS IN SELECTING A PROFESSIONAL DEVELOPMENT MODEL

The continuum of professional development models presented in Figure 2.1 is representative of the options available to professional development planners and teachers. Each model may be useful to achieve certain types of goals; thus, a number of factors need to be considered in selecting a professional development model.

Goals of Professional Development

The primary consideration in selecting a professional development model is the nature of the goal that one wants to achieve. For example, informational activities require little in the way of preparation and planning and are most efficiently accomplished through single-day large-group gatherings. Although such activities can hardly be called *professional development*, they are nonetheless useful for disseminating information. Complex issues such as raising test scores in reading and mathematics require greater teacher involvement and a more significant time and resource commitment to accomplish.

Human and Financial Resources

One real-world fact is that professional development requires school board and administrative support. Appropriate allocation of human and financial resources is necessary for an effective professional development program. Providing appropriate team planning time when all members of the team are available during the same period can be a challenge to many schools. Administrators must make a commitment to utilizing techniques such as creative scheduling and use of appropriate staff to provide teachers with the necessary time during the school day to work in teams. At times, outside experts may be required to help move a particular professional development initiative along. Both the school board and the administration must be committed to providing a vibrant professional development program that enhances teachers' personal and professional development needs, achieves school district goals, enhances student learning, and results in observable improvements.

Interpersonal Relationships

Collaborative and team-based professional development require interpersonal relationships that foster team building. Not only is collaboration a component of the National Staff Development Council standards, but it has been shown to be the most effective way of actively involving teachers in professional development activities that lead to systemic reform. Carefully evaluating the mix of personalities among the teaching staff is an important step in determining team composition. In observations of previous collaborative and team-based professional development efforts, it is clear that such interaction has the power to reinvigorate teachers' careers and set them on a path to self-improvement.

In the past, teachers have not sought out collaborative, team-based relationships with their colleagues. Learning to work together in small teams is a new skill that must be nurtured. Providing initial training in teamwork along with periodic coaching enhances the likelihood of success and of developing long-term habits that lead to ongoing professional development that is teacher driven, goal oriented, and focused on data-driven and research-based decision making.

Collaborative, team-based professional development is an adaptable model that can meet many needs. Acquiring knowledge, changing attitudes, and developing skills are the essence of professional development. To achieve any or all of the above may require substantially different approaches to professional development determined by the objectives. One-day in-service programs have their place—but do not be deluded into thinking that such an approach changes attitudes or develops skills. To do so requires one of the options further along the continuum, where there is greater teacher involvement.

In planning effective professional development programs, educators (administrators and teachers) must agree on the goals, develop a comprehensive action plan to achieve those goals (including the allocation of necessary resources), and systematically collect appropriate data to evaluate the extent to which the goals are achieved. Selection of the appropriate model for accomplishing the goals is an important part of the process.

3

Teachers Who Asked *What If?* Criteria for Successful Team-Based Professional Development

"You want me to *what*? How can I think about teaming when I need to prepare my classes for the state assessment?"

"I wish we could find some in-service plan that would allow us all to work together toward getting these juniors ready for the state PSSAs [Pennsylvania System of School Assessment, a standards-based criterion-referenced assessment used to measure a student's attainment of the academic standards while also determining the degree to which school programs enable students to attain proficiency of the standards]. I am so busy drilling information into them that I think I sometimes forget the reason I went into education. I pictured working together with other teachers like I did my last year of college before we went out student teaching. Here I feel so alone most of the time."

"I wish I had known that most of my students also had a major project due for Mrs. Walton the same day their research paper was due for me. If she had said something to me—but then we don't have the same planning period or lunch period and I tutor after school, so I never see her. I would have changed the date mine was due, or better yet, maybe we could have worked together so that some aspect of their civics project could have been their English research topic."

"Some days I feel that I am locked up in my room and am the only adult in the building because I rarely ever see another teacher."

"Jerry, I am so tired of the same old in-service days. Remember how great the unit was that you, Louise, Bill, and I worked on at my house the summer before last? We felt so energized and said we thought that this is what the Steve Jobs' model of a skunkworks must have been like. I am hearing from the freshmen in college how often they think about that unit and they tell me that while it took them a little while to realize it, they did learn that all learning is interconnected."

Teachers rarely have such feedback as this, and even when they do, they have little power or authority to analyze what factors made a teaching unit successful, let alone try to trace that success to a particular in-service program. So many factors enter into a change such as the one that occurred with the teachers who spent time together one summer that it would be hard for them to identify anything except the fact that they had planned the unit together. Likewise, it is difficult to determine if particular professional development efforts are effective in a given school. The potential influences and factors on its success are infinite. To complicate matters, the number and kinds of professional development initiatives that schools simultaneously undertake at all levels and areas of teaching and learning can be daunting and easily lost track of. So much is happening in schools that a few years following a successful program, few people can remember why it was successful, and they often attribute it to chance.

Faculty often perceive that an increasing array of curriculum initiatives are added each year with no realistic adjustment in expectations for teachers and with little connection to what they are currently doing or what was emphasized by the administration the previous year. In addition, schools have multiple program initiatives for which they are responsible—for example, violence prevention, multicultural awareness, energy conservation, gender issues, community service—but which are not part of the standardized testing programs by which school success is judged. Add to this list the mandates of the No Child Left Behind Act and its accompanying accountability, which affect schools' ratings (to say nothing of the pressure placed on the classroom teachers), and there is much potential for frustration. All of these initiatives and mandates dilute the precious time that teachers have available for teaching the content and concepts they deem important. This is often why the last thing that teachers want to hear about is professional development, even if it promises to make their lives easier, offers them personal empowerment, and increases their students' scores in the state academic assessments.

Although student achievement is considered the educational bottom line, it cannot always be the most important measure by which the effectiveness of professional development efforts is determined. To do so creates a simplistic view of the purpose of professional development. Without question, the long-range goals of professional development should affect student achievement, but the outcomes of successful professional development are multidimensional and aimed at myriad improvements, including increased professionalism and satisfaction among faculty (to say nothing of the positive effects of enthusiasm), better school climate, richer content, and a deeper classroom engagement between teachers and students.

IMPORTANT COMPONENTS LEADING TO SUCCESS

Surprising to some educators are the studies that have confirmed that the amount of time that teachers spend in professional development is not significantly relevant to student achievement but that the content and instruction of the courses are (Garet et al., 2001). In other words, more time spent in professional development of poor quality will not improve student achievement, but highly focused professional development that targets teachers' content knowledge and content-specific instructional practices will (Shulman, 1986; Wenglinsky, 2000). Other research has added that professional development that is coherent and sustained and that focuses on student achievement, engages students, incorporates higher-order thinking, and builds a learning community produces results for both teachers and students (Garet et al., 2001; McCaffrey et al., 2001; McLaughlin & Talbert, 2001; Wenglinsky, 2000). Significantly, Newmann, King, and Youngs (2000) found that individual teacher learning is insufficient to produce results on its own. The learning must happen in settings on-site that promote collaboration and shared learning (Fullan, 2001). Changing the context of schools to create settings for building and sharing learning among adults is essential to produce learning for students (Killion, 2002). This finding means "that teachers and principals work together to identify and solve complex problems . . . not with simple, easy-to-implement strategies recommended by those outside the school, but with answers that they construct for *themselves*" (p. 19).

There is literature delineating the roles of teachers and administrators in school reform (e.g., Bredeson, 1992; Page, 1994; Patterson, 1993), as well as what is necessary for providing a successful organizational climate to support that reform (e.g., Fullan, 1991; Osborne, 1993a, 1993b). This literature has provided a variety of viewpoints from which to identify the factors that contribute to successful school reform. Rarely, however, are districts able to have in place all factors that are identified in the research literature. Determining which components are merely desirable and which are essential is the key to effectively establishing a successful team-based professional development program.

As many school districts across the country are undertaking important curriculum reform initiatives and supporting professional development efforts, knowledge of factors that enhance the chances of success becomes increasingly important. A number of research articles have reported the success of programs that implemented some type of curriculum reform (e.g., Peters et al., 1995; Wepner, 1993a, 1993b; Williams & Reynolds, 1993). More than 20 different factors can be found that suggest how success can be attained only when all of these factors are firmly in place. These factors include human and financial resources, various teacher and administrator characteristics, and a number of team-building issues. Yet several school districts have demonstrated their capacity to successfully initiate and sustain professional development and curriculum reform in less-than-ideal circumstances. For example, through a statewide curriculum integration project involving 11 school districts, ongoing professional development and the curriculum reform process were examined to determine which factors, or which combination of factors, were essential for success (Melnick & Schubert, 1997; Melnick & Witmer, 1999).

Programs were considered successful if they accomplished their project goals, developed sustainable structure, and institutionalized team-based processes. Through a comparison of the programs and their respective levels of success, it is clear that although a number of the characteristics found in the literature enhance success (enablers), only a subset of these factors are essential elements (disablers), without which programs are far less successful in their efforts. Assessing the relative importance of these tangible and intangible factors and determining which factors simply enhance the chances of success (enablers) and which factors are crucial to success (disablers) are important steps toward widespread and sustainable systemic reform.

The following sections describe team-based professional development and the five common elements that we have found necessary for successful professional development (disablers). Examples are provided, as well as evidence of validation for the model.

TEAM-BASED PROFESSIONAL DEVELOPMENT

Team-based professional development is a model whereby small teams of teachers with common interests help one another learn about their own learning; study and reflect on their own teaching; develop ongoing, sustained professional relationships with each other; and take responsibility for their professional growth and development. Previous research has identified a number of factors crucial to success that provide the greatest possibility for these initiatives to take root and become successful. Factors identified in the literature that delineate the roles of teachers and administrators in school reform (e.g., Peters et al., 1995; Wepner, 1993a, 1993b; Williams & Reynolds, 1993) and foster a successful organizational climate (e.g., Fullan, 1991; Osborne, 1993a, 1993b) were considered in later studies by Melnick and Schubert (1997) and the two of us (Witmer & Melnick, 1997), which laid the groundwork for the team-based professional development model.

Melnick and Schubert (1997) looked at 23 factors noted in the literature as being important to successful professional development and curriculum initiatives. These can be broadly categorized into five areas: administrative involvement, communication, curriculum issues, resources, and teacher teaming (see Table 3.1). Interviews conducted in 11 school districts revealed that the 23 factors were found to be enablers—factors that, if in place, enhanced the process and provided the greatest opportunity for success. However, contrary to the literature, not all of these factors were found to be absolutely necessary for success. That is, a number of districts had exciting and successful programs even though many of the factors were absent. As it turns out, there were factors common to all the programs that, *without which*, the district efforts were significantly diminished or doomed to failure (disablers).

Critical factors such as provision of adequate resources (particularly, time to work together), teacher teaming, organizational support, communication, and curriculum were found to be essential to success

Table 3.1. Factors Contributing to Institutionalizing Curriculum Reform

Administrator Involvement	Building Administrator Central office Superintendent
Communication	Other teachers Administrators Board members Parents Community
Curriculum issues	Clear goals Curriculum revisions Curriculum model utilized (specific)
Resources	Team planning time Professional development Money Common students Released time to meet and plan
Teacher teaming	Cooperation among teachers Personal commitment on the part of teachers Empowering teachers to design, shape, implement curricular change Size Philosophy Volunteers Leadership

and were present in the five most successful sites. The remaining six sites, less successful in their project efforts, were lacking in one or more of the five areas. The following includes a definition of each of the five areas listed in Table 3.1:

1. *Administrative involvement* is basic to the success of the team. Administrators must provide creative solutions to the unique challenges of team-based professional development (e.g., scheduling to provide common planning time), and they must plan the necessary time to stay actively involved in the project.
2. *Communication* to all constituencies is necessary. Keeping students, colleagues, administrators, and parents fully informed of curriculum changes, instructional improvements, assignments, and expectations is an essential part of professional develop-

ment efforts. Effective communication promotes teamwork among teachers, fosters administrative support, provides for informed decision making by the board, and keeps the community informed.

3. *Curriculum issues* drive the process—namely, curriculum revisions. For those revisions to become systemic reforms, clear goals that are owned by everyone involved are essential. The goals keep everyone on track and focused to help ensure the highest levels of accomplishment. One technique found to be helpful is to develop an acronym, like TILT (Teaching, Integrating, Learning Together), that makes the project's goals (not the project's name) easy to remember so that students, teachers, administrators, and parents focus on accomplishing them.

4. *Resources* are required. All involved need to find creative ways to reallocate resources, financial and human, that are essential to ensure success without significantly increasing costs. Time is the most important resource. Teams need time together during the school day to plan, implement, and reflect. What some of the teams found surprising is that even small financial commitments to their efforts resulted in large gains.

5. *Teacher teaming* is a necessary and evolving process that requires everyone to be a part of it; shared ownership is crucial to success. All involved need to recognize the necessity of forming teams of teachers who identify critical issues in need of improvement and solutions to existing problems and who overcome obstacles to find ways to make a difference for their students. Teachers need to hold or develop a shared vision for school improvement, and this vision must be defined.

Based on previous research (Melnick & Schubert, 1997; Witmer & Melnick, 1997) regarding the effectiveness of team-based professional development, further research was conducted that (a) assessed the perceptions of teachers regarding their professional development along five constructs (teaming, time, organizational support, communication, and professional responsibility) and (b) compared the perceptions of teachers utilizing a team-based approach to professional development, with the perceptions of their colleagues who did not (Melnick & Witmer, 1999). The results of that study led to the refinement of the team-based professional development model.

ADMINISTRATIVE INVOLVEMENT

It is often thought that strong instructional leadership on the part of the building principal is necessary and sufficient for curricular change. This study focused on issues related to the leadership provided by the building principal in addition to central office personnel. Where sites were most successful, administrators at all levels were willing to share decision-making responsibility with the teacher teams. Not only were these administrators supportive, but they were actively involved in the process. For instance, building the schedule around teachers' instructional needs demonstrated the respect that the building principal had for teachers as professionals. These principals were secure in their role and did not feel threatened by teachers' input into traditionally administrative issues—scheduling, for example. There seemed to be a symbiotic relationship between teachers and administrators that was uncharacteristic at other, less successful sites.

However, building-level administrative involvement was not sufficient by itself. Although in the most successful sites the superintendent was knowledgeable about the project and its goals, sites that did not have the active support and involvement of the district curriculum director were far less successful. At both the building and the central office level, being merely supportive was not sufficient. Administrators at all levels needed to play an active role and be intimately involved in the process. For example, one district's assistant superintendent for curriculum was supportive of a school's efforts to integrate the arts into other areas of the curriculum. As a school with a culturally diverse population, the team planned a central theme focusing on harvest traditions of different cultures, and it used a garden on the school grounds to involve the elementary-age children in a hands-on learning experience. Unfortunately, the garden was vandalized, but because of the assistant superintendent's active involvement and commitment to the project, he was able to find funding to construct a chain-link fence around the garden. Ten years later, that school is still using its garden as part of its instructional program. That is not to say that the teachers could not have presented a case to the administration for the expenditure of funds; rather, it illustrates that with the intervention by the assistant superintendent, fewer hurdles were encountered while providing the necessary resources to keep the project going and the enthusiasm high.

Contributing to the overall organizational climate, the school board played a pivotal role at each site. Although not involved in the day-to-day operation of the various team initiatives, the board's support (verbal, if not financial) was important to the teachers. Not only did it create an atmosphere in which their teachers' expertise was valued, but it exemplified an attitude of professionalism that permeated the district.

CURRICULUM ISSUES

The area of curriculum issues focused on those issues related directly to the district's curriculum and instruction. Three issues were of interest: the extent to which clear goals had been specified and understood by the team members; the extent to which the team was able to work within the existing curriculum framework or undergo significant revisions; and, finally, the extent to which teams understood and utilized existing models through their own research.

The most successful sites had clear, specific goals for their projects. One site reported, "The very first thing we did was to figure out exactly what we wanted to accomplish." It seemed a logical, commonsense thing to do, yet it was a deliberate part of the process. The less successful sites were characterized by a good bit of initial confusion. In a school where teachers were unclear of the goals, one participant stated, "I was confused in the beginning because I didn't know what the focus was supposed to be." Such reports were commonplace among these sites.

The successful sites incorporated as much of their existing curriculum as possible into their integrated units. They tried to "fit some existing areas together first" and were "building more each year" into their units. They did not expend energy and resources on making major changes to the curriculum but instead focused their energies on designing integrated units and instruction around current content and available materials. Although the less successful sites intended to utilize the existing curriculum, they found themselves creating a host of new materials and incorporating new content. Because of the tremendous amounts of time expended in this manner, the less productive sites were unfocused and weary of the process.

Additionally, teachers who sought out the latest research to guide and support their teaching had an understanding of why particular strategies worked and why others failed. The most successful teams were actively engaged in action research and were continually evaluating their teaching in light of current research in the field and successful curriculum and instruction models. It was clear that they kept up with reading professional journals and, as a result, understood and respected the theories that supported their instruction. All of the effective teams exhibited a high degree of professionalism, and four of the five most effective teams participated in professional conference presentations.

COMMUNICATION

Communicating about curriculum reform efforts clearly distinguished successful sites from unsuccessful sites. In districts who successfully institutionalized their reform efforts, teacher teams and administrators made a concerted effort to communicate the goals and objectives, methods, and outcomes with other constituencies. Teams made presentations to their colleagues during district in-service days. There was significantly improved and frequent communication between teachers and administrators. Teachers and students made presentations to board members to keep them informed of the progress being made. Letters and news bulletins were sent home to parents, and frequent coverage of school activities was published by the local newspapers. The mere act of notifying the newspaper of school activities is probably less significant than the underlying reasons that teachers do so. Communicating their successes brings important positive attention to the team, the students, and the work that they all are doing. Teachers who notify the newspaper are proud of their students' accomplishments and their own, and they believe that what they all are doing is noteworthy. Such recognition validates the importance of the profession and the contributions made by teachers. The teachers in this study had an understanding of the power of the media and sought to use it in a positive way. In short, by keeping all constituencies well informed, the team generated understanding and support.

RESOURCES

The area of resources focused on concerns that had a direct impact on human and financial resources. Examples include released time for teachers, direct expenditures for materials, costs associated with professional development, and staffing implications for creating schedules that allow for common planning time and common students for team members. This area is significant in that it requires all concerned to find ways to creatively reallocate resources. Aspects of ongoing professional development efforts often require the expenditure of funds, or they have staffing implications and consequently necessitate both central office and building-level administrative support.

The most significant factor in this area is time. Time has typically been the elusive element in unsuccessful professional development efforts and the reason why other worthy initiatives have not succeeded. The districts that were most successful placed a priority on including planning time in their days and demonstrated a commitment to the success of the project by redesigning schedules in creative ways to generate the necessary common times. In one elementary school, for example, the schedule was designed in such a way that all children at one grade level had classes with teachers of special subjects (art, music, physical education, etc.) during the same period. As a result, the regular classroom teachers were able to meet as a team. The unfortunate side of this rescheduling is that the teachers of the special subjects were not included in the team meetings. Although not ideal, the new schedule was nonetheless a step in the right direction and demonstrated administrative commitment to the process. In another school, class sizes were slightly increased to allow for one fewer scheduled period every other day—this period became the team planning time. As one administrator said, "You simply have got to give teachers time among themselves to sit down and plan during the school. It is unrealistic to expect them to do it all on their own time."

Interestingly, not all teacher teams had time scheduled as part of the school day to meet. Where teachers were not provided with common planning time by the district, programs struggled to be successful. However, in the case of a few very focused teams where the district was unable to provide common planning time, teachers created it. In fact, most felt so strong about the importance of team planning that they made time to meet as a team. Many had informal meetings before and after school, met with brown bags during their scheduled lunchtimes, or in some cases got together on a few Saturdays for planning purposes. These teachers strongly believed in collaboration and were self-confident in their own right. They viewed the sharing of instructional strategies and ideas as an important part of their own professional growth.

Although all sites were given the same amount of grant funding, those sites that were most successful used a greater portion of the funds to purchase released time for teachers by hiring substitute teachers for a day, allowing all team members to be free to meet; the less successful sites tended to purchase "things" (e.g., books, computer programs, supplies) rather than time. The observed difference among the sites in this regard was clear: Teachers used this released time to meet in teams, attend professional development activities, and make presentations to others (colleagues, board members, parents, and the community) about their successes. The less successful teams spent their available resources on fine collections of resource materials but never really had the time to carefully plan how to use them.

In addition, the most successful sites received additional resources from the central administration or other sources. There were a small number of teams that sought out and received external grant funding ranging from $500 to $25,000. These funds were used to augment existing curriculum and provide opportunities for planning and instruction that would otherwise not have occurred.

Although districts should attempt to provide for each of the factors in this area, the lack of time was clearly the disabling factor for the less successful sites. Freeing up financial and human resources and judiciously allocating them to accomplish project goals is crucial to successful professional development efforts.

TEACHER TEAMING

This area focused on issues related to the working relationships and commitment of the teachers involved in the project. The key factors in the teaming included the degree of cooperation among teachers; personal commitment to the professional development project on the part of teachers; and the empowerment of teachers to design, shape, and implement changes. The size of the team, its shared vision (i.e., philosophy), volunteer status, and leadership were also considered in the study.

Without exception, successful teams saw the advantage of working together to not only share instructional strategies but also take advantage of one another's strengths. They held a belief that teaming enriched the content and enhanced its delivery. Teachers reported increased student interaction and saw gains in achievement. Teachers who team-taught were self-confident.

Not surprisingly, personal commitment on the part of the teachers is crucial. Perhaps it is one of the most intriguing factors, because it is clear that a chemistry difficult to quantify needs to exist among team members. Teams with the most successful projects were characterized by excellent cooperation and a feeling of collegiality. They seemed to get along well, both professionally and socially. It also was clear that these teachers had contact with one another beyond the school day. The less successful teams, however, appeared to have no contact among themselves beyond normal school hours. In discussing the bond among team members, one teacher stated, "I think we've always had good relationships, but I think we've become closer and bond more now because we're in this together. It's been fun; it really has!" A central office administrator characterized the teaming concept succinctly by saying, "What it boils down to is the ability of people to work and interact together as a collective unit." Without the collective trust and collegiality, any reform is doomed from the start. The importance of team building cannot be underestimated, because not only do the benefits ensure success in professional development efforts but they also have a reenergizing effect on teachers. As one teacher reported,

> I don't feel isolated as a classroom teacher any more. I felt really strong professional relationships were established and that input was given back and forth between people who never before even came into my classroom. I found myself teaching art lessons and the art teacher found herself teaching about writing. It was a nice blend rather than always being isolated—a really nice camaraderie developed among us.

Although each of the factors in this area contributed to successful teams, a lack of commitment, empowerment, or a common philosophy derailed the initiative in less successful districts. One of the most successful sites in the project spent the entire first year building the commitment and developing a common philosophy while all the time empowering teachers to make changes. Sites that did not have these three teacher-teaming factors in common (commitment, philosophy, and empowerment) were destined to be unsuccessful.

This research demonstrates that of the more than 20 factors that contribute to successful professional development leading to systemic change, 5 specific factors were essential: administrative involvement, communication, curriculum revisions, resources, and effective teacher teaming. Because professional development is a major thrust in school reform efforts, this research underscores the importance of teachers working in teams toward a common goal, having the support of both the school board and the administration to be creative and launch initiatives, and communicating about their successes. Taking the time to work in teams was also an important factor in distinguishing the effective teams from the noneffective. Most important is an understanding of why and how the five most successful sites worked together and how other districts can initiate and sustain such teambased professional development in a variety of settings.

Given the expense of school reform efforts and the consequences of failure, every effort should be made to ensure success. It is apparent that districts will be better able to effect school reform and enhance ongoing professional development by concentrating on the factors most important to success. A school site that is considering implementing team-based professional development will benefit from following the guidelines of this model while taking into account the culture of its own institution. By beginning with a willing team—one comprising teachers who are confident in their performance; who have demonstrated success in the classroom; and who respect one another's skills, knowledge, and points of view—a school will find it easy to support team-based professional development. The effort expended will be well worth it because the results will exponentially benefit the school, the team, and the students.

4

Can You Do This?
Successful Programs

All of us who ever taught high school have known Frank. His name may have been George or Pete or Harry, but we knew him the minute that he stepped inside our classrooms. There was a certain attitude, a posture, sometimes even a smirk. Our Frank might have been deferential in that mocking sort of way that cannot be defined and reported as a disciplinary problem, or he might have just sulked in a seat in the last row, surly and unresponsive. He might have been a quiet instigator, goading others to be disruptive, or he might simply have been passively resistant. Whatever his mode of operation, he was definitely not interested in school.

Frank, a real student at one of our high school sites in the Keystone Integrated Framework Project, was this typical noninvolved, antagonistic student. Some called him a "hellion," others "the class clown." None of his teachers disliked him; they saw him for what they thought he was and tolerated him as best they could. Each teacher, in turn, tried her or his best techniques to interest Frank in the task at hand. The teaching team in the Keystone project wondered aloud just why Frank would have elected to take this particular humanities course, the only class in the school identified as an elective. No one had forced him to self-select this team-taught pilot course, yet there he was, every day, a presence with which to be reckoned.

The one positive that Frank had going for him was his interest in art. Among the students enrolled in this humanities course, Frank was the only student who had elected to take a class in the visual arts. This art course helped Frank to develop some technical understanding, refinement of skill, and factual information that the other students in the humanities class did not possess. No one thought much about the fact that Frank was taking both courses, because most of the teachers' interaction with him involved trying to interest him in the humanities project and not in amusing the other students.

Then one day when the students were having difficulty understanding a corollary between visual art and literary art, Frank spoke. As he began to use concepts such as analysis and interpretation about works of art, students and teachers began to see him in a new light. From that time forward, other students began to seek him out, asking for his help. Frank became able to draw on his talent and understanding previously displayed in only his art class, to make the needed connections between art and academics. To everyone's astonishment and delight, for the first time Frank began to take his academic work seriously. He soon became a better student in all of his classes, a success where he might once have been a failure.

THE KEYSTONE INTEGRATED FRAMEWORK PROJECT

The Keystone Integrated Framework Project, a 3-year federally funded program, was an initiative promoting the integration of curriculum—specifically, the integration of the arts with civics, English, geography, and history. Eleven Pennsylvania school sites who partnered with higher education institutions were selected through a competitive request for proposals to serve as pilot sites for the project. One criterion for selection was the commitment from each site to develop a unit or program on curriculum integration. Members of these pilot sites initially attended a week-long retreat (Summer Institute) in August 1995 where they received intensive training in teaming, as well as guidance in planning their programs.

This is the story of seven schools who represent the project. Six of these schools illustrate successful implementation of the team-based professional development model (even though the term *team-based professional development* was not used in the framework process), and one school does not. Although the latter school was not successful in the traditional sense, it is one whose team showed fortitude against overwhelming odds. Each team from these seven Pennsylvania schools was comprised of four to nine teachers and, with the exception of the seventh site, an administrator. Seen among the seven sites are examples of horizontal teams (those across classrooms in the same grade level) and vertical teams (those across grade levels). (Characteristics of these programs are found in Table 3.1, to delineate what characteristics led to their success. The table may also be helpful in identifying and associating components in common with the reader's own school.)

Nothing is as powerful as the words of those who actually lived the Keystone Integrated Framework Project experience of pioneering curriculum integration through collaborative, team-based professional development. Most participants came to the project with energy, desire, and commitment. All were risk takers, having no idea of what they were getting into, but they believed in themselves and in the ability of their students. Some had been involved in various school reform initiatives, and, although a few were admittedly skeptical because they had "done this before," all retained a fresh optimism that there were better ways to teach and learn. What most participants did not realize at the initial stages of this project is that they were experiencing team-based professional development and were a part of a community of learners who had not yet found that community.

MOUNTAIN VIEW JUNIOR–SENIOR HIGH SCHOOL

Nothing important ever happens in Susquehanna County.
What a dumb place to live. Why do people stay here?
This was a challenge the teachers in this rural community could not ignore.

The teachers at Mountain View Junior–Senior High School exemplify what can be accomplished through collaboration when there is a strong will to make it work. Geographically and culturally isolated on a tertiary road, rural Mountain View is the home to 750 students in Grades 7–12. The townships that make up the school district all have small populations who farm, own their own businesses, or commute to jobs in larger cities. We begin this chapter with four teachers—one in visual arts, one in theater and English, one in social studies, and one in library and research—who shared a vision of collaboration and succeeded by making an enormous impact on their school and their county by committing themselves to the concept, and then the reality, of making themselves a team.

Admittedly naïve enough to not realize just how much work there would be, the teachers began with an idea that they had talked about among only themselves. They had a dream to create an elective humanities class that would be team-taught, and they hoped a grant might help them forge it into reality. Even with a supportive new principal, the four core teachers were faced with no common planning time, no students whom they all had in common, and no space of their own; further, what they did have was students ranging in Grades 9–12, students meeting in different periods per day, and a local university partner that was unable to keep its initial commitment to provide training and help with curriculum planning and implementation. Despite these barriers, the Mountain View teachers decided to make their own way, meeting early in the morning, chatting over lunch on the days when at least three of the four were scheduled at the same time, and grabbing a few minutes in the hall together. They were on their own—except for a week during the summer when they were immersed in planning as a team under the tutelage of facilitators provided through the Keystone federal grant.

From that near-formless beginning, the Mountain View team developed a yearlong integrated course of study titled Culture Shock for students in Grades 9–12. This course was intended to make students aware of the local county culture and have them develop an appreciation for their regional heritage. Students were invited to investigate various aspects of life in their county and engage in a variety of research activities to learn about the history, geography, art, architecture, folklore, music, and business and technology that surrounded them in their own community. Students produced, as a culminating event, a video documentary of their findings.

Through classroom meetings with the instructor of the day, the students played a major role in focusing the course content to make it relevant to their lives. They explored local and county government, industry and tourism, and folk and primitive art, finishing the year by focusing on aesthetics. Through the incorporation of music, theater, and visual arts, students came to understand the meaning and importance of the arts in their lives and culture.

As word of the Culture Shock class spread through the school, high school faculty who were not initially involved in the project volunteered their expertise. Community leaders, the school superintendent, and representatives from business and tourism contributed to the students' understanding of their county. The teacher team discovered the added benefit of taking students out of school to visit the county historical society, the courthouse, the library, the forestry office, the 4-H office, and the county extension office, the latter two organizations being very familiar in this farming community. The students also traveled to neighboring counties to explore their histories and cultures and their impact on the students' county. In the process, they developed relationships with individuals in the local artists' colony and the local churches and historical societies.

In-class teacher instruction and lecture were kept to a minimum, and students used class time to write, research, discuss, plan, interview, and videotape. However, one of the most important lessons that the teachers learned was the disadvantage of separate consultations with students, who quickly noted differences in what each teacher told them. This loose interpretation of what they were being told caused great consternation among the students, and the team members soon realized that they had to develop a shared concept of each assignment so that the direction they gave the students would be clear, precise, and consistent. As one teacher later said, "It took a good deal of discussion and compromise and growth for us to get this aspect of our team effort in order."

The team noted that the most impressive aspect of this class was the transformation of the students from passive to active learners: The students owned their work. They became independent learners and applied skills learned in this project to other areas of study. The project made dancers from athletes, visual artists from reluctant scientists, and primary source researchers from encyclopedia hounds. Most of all, they made believers of skeptics.

CLARION ELEMENTARY /
CLARION UNIVERSITY

I've been party to many reform efforts over the years, and most have been pretty disappointing, but this one was different. People came together, collaborated, changed the way things were done, and felt good about it. Parents liked it, too. One of my students asked me what to put on the heading of his paper. We had always placed the name of the subject directly under the student's name, so I asked him, "Well, what do you think should be placed there?" The child paused, thinking, and after a few seconds replied, wise for his years, "I guess we should just call it learning!"

A small school district in western Pennsylvania, Clarion Elementary School is located in the county seat whose major industry is a state university. Clarion focused its work on Grades 3–8 as part of the social studies curriculum. Working with the four team members from Clarion University, the six school team members from the elementary school, representing each of the grades in the project, chose an area of the basic social studies curriculum to develop and expand.

Highlights of the collaborative team-based professional development in Clarion Elementary School included an unflappable building principal, strong parental support, and a solid university partnership. Clarion University, with its commitment to outreach programs to neighboring local schools, found a perfect partner in Clarion Elementary School, located only blocks from the education building on campus. With a history of placing student teachers in the local school and an attractive master's program in which many of the local teachers were enrolled, a close partnership was soon formed.

Collaborative planning began with a 1-week workshop before a week's training with all other teams in the Keystone project. As one team member commented, "We've learned so much from one another. Educators seldom get a time like this to share ideas with a definite goal in mind. We've gained a lot of insight into the realities of what each of us does. I can see how we will all benefit from closer collaboration."

An unusual feature of Clarion's project is that a team member taught seventh grade at the high school. The seventh-grade children wrote and published their own books about Pennsylvania, and the seventh-grade team member brought his students to the elementary school, where they read their books to the fourth graders.

Shortly into the first year of the project, the other teachers in the building could not help but notice the enthusiasm and excitement of the teachers and children involved in the project. One teacher commented that even though the Civil War unit was over, the children still were interested in learning more about it. Teachers reported that the work that students had done during the time of the project was by far the most outstanding work they had seen all year.

The teachers and university partners met on a regular basis, becoming friends as well as colleagues in the process of their planning, and student teachers developed integrated units during their methods semester and used them during student teaching. Collaboration and team planning were expanded through a link with an urban Keystone project site in Philadelphia, culminating in exchange visits and collaborative teaching. The teachers exchanged materials, and the children exchanged letters and photos, all learning the similarities and differences between urban and rural schools.

Parents also became active supporters of the project. During the unit on the pioneers of the westward movement, for example, one of the fathers constructed a Conestoga wagon. He built it so that it could be assembled and disassembled, to use as needed. Once the wagon was set up in the classroom, the children were able to climb on it and use it as a reading nook. Teachers noted many instances in which parents sought them out to comment positively on the curriculum units. Parents reported that they had never before seen their children so excited about a school project.

CONESTOGA VALLEY MIDDLE SCHOOL / MILLERSVILLE UNIVERSITY

In early June, all eight of us met in the middle school's weathered seminar room in an aging building, and after several minutes of stilted conversation, teachers and university faculty spent 2 hours trying to get to know one another. We were all educators with diverse learning styles and agendas who couldn't be as different from each other unless it were planned, yet we all had the same goal—we wanted to create a memorable experience for our students. Once the intensive planning started, the problems started, too. We met, we worked, we brainstormed, we argued, we planned, we fought, and we started from scratch all over again. We knew where we wanted to go but not how we were going to get there.

Conestoga Valley, a middle school in comfortable upper-middle-class suburbia, refined a simulation that they had piloted for a problem-solving unit for an eighth-grade team. Supported by their administration, this faculty team was a smooth-running collaborative unit. The key to its success was the rapport among colleagues and with their students. In addition, they were blessed with a university partnership that provided professional support, friendship, preservice teachers, and university student helpers. The middle school teachers had successfully worked together as a team for several years; this was their strength as well as their weakness, because with their past successes came a certain hubris.

Their systematic approach to the project included a prepared manual clearly outlining all of the project's expectations. It detailed individual assessments, group assessments, and required performances. The manual served as a guide to the students and introduced them to a project style of problem solving unfamiliar to most of them. As an introduction to the project, the students were presented with a clever scenario and charged with developing solutions:

> Picture, if you will, the year 2113. Earth is on the verge of disaster—pollution, drugs, and violence have snowballed. Humans, in order to survive, are moving to new habitats called "cylinders" in outer space. Although the habitats were set up to get away from the problems of society on Earth, it wasn't long until each cylinder was "infected" with one of the problems humans sought to get away from.

To solve the problems in this scenario, the students had to complete four tasks. First, they had to identify and explain the specific problem. Second, using one or more media of the visual arts, they had to convince the population that the problem existed and needed to be solved. Third, they had to propose a solution via the auditory arts. Fourth, using any presentation mode of their choosing, they had to predict what the future would be like in their cylinders.

Excited with the enthusiasm of the middle school teachers and vowing to *work with* rather than *deliver to*, the university partners viewed the project as the opportunity to begin an integration of courses into their teacher preparation program that they had been talking about for years. That plan included working collaboratively with colleagues in the delivery of curriculum in their university courses, providing an unusual and valuable experience for student teachers, and working as members of an authentic team in a public school. Through the project, this plan was able to become a reality.

However, even with such an opportunity, teaming at a university is a far more formidable task than that in a self-contained school building, and this university team had taken on the additional challenge of teaming not only with the education faculty but also with other departments, including those of art, music, and technology. The education professors decided that the best way to approach teaming was to first walk across the campus and meet on the turf of the other departments. Their second step was to have all potential faculty team members meet over lunch in the common dining hall. The third was to seek outcomes that were win–win for all participants. Their overall discussions were driven by three goals: one, to bridge across schools, courses, and schedules in a way that student teachers could learn to teach and work with middle school students; two, to build new connections and strengthen existing bonds; and, three, to improve the student teachers' education program. A core team was agreed on, and its members attended the week-long team-training retreat with the school team.

This retreat was a new experience for most university faculty, to spend a week in a remote mountain resort with the sole mission of leaving with a plan for an integrated curriculum unit in a school—a plan that would greatly affect the curriculum and scheduling at the university, as well as those of the school. As the two groups moved forward that week and in successive planning meetings—both with the other project sites and with their own team members—a shift in view occurred and, with it, fewer demands by each side (teachers and university faculty) and even a decrease in the use of the word *compromise*. Instead, all were planning the same goal: to provide an enriching experience for the eighth graders and the student teachers, who would be graduated with invaluable experience in teaming. What began as two teams—university professors who had not worked together before and middle school teachers who already had formed bonds— became one team with one mind, one goal, and one voice.

What the professors found most exciting was that they were shaping a strong connection between the lives of future teachers and a real world of the public school in a middle school where they could observe and participate in cutting-edge exemplary instruction. What was most challenging was the scheduling of the arts and technology students as observers and student specialists so that their college classes would not be scheduled at the same time as the eighth-grade project class periods.

There were unanticipated problems, mainly that teachers and professors had underestimated both the volume of work and the amount of rehearsal time needed for the culminating event of the project, a presentation to the entire middle school. The mantra of the team became "Each day we learn a little more." And they did.

DONEGAL AREA MIDDLE SCHOOL / MILLERSVILLE UNIVERSITY

But our director of transportation has spent weeks on making the bus schedule work, and now you are telling me that your eighth graders are saying that they can plan a more efficient bus routing system?

Strong central office support was the hallmark of Donegal's project. From replacing a solid wall between two classrooms with a folding one to arranging for a long-term substitute to release the music teacher for the special curriculum unit, administrative support at all levels ensured a smooth road for students and teachers. This commitment provided a caring environment for finding creative and workable solutions to student-identified problems, the focus of Donegal's project.

In their own words they wrote,

> On Sunday, August 13, several cars headed north. . . . The building itself foreshadowed the coming gloom and strife that would mark our group's first hours together.
>
>   Despite the first night's gathering, which was a mixer for all participants and included a not universally welcomed improvisational dance exercise, the first day's work involved the laying out of "various ideas, some suitcases, a few boxes of what we had thought were related materials, and some golf clubs." It became quite evident after a short discussion that our group would not be able to come to a conclusion during this meeting. Our original idea of an African American theme was not meeting with consensus from our group of university professors and Donegal teachers. As the meeting continued, roles began to emerge. Five members had a preconceived idea as to the direction we would follow. One thought seriously of packing up and going home. Two tried to keep the group connected, whereas the remainder focused on their own visions, oblivious to the turmoil in the minds of the others. By the end of the day we left the "Friendship Room" wondering whether our friendships would weather the storm of teaming.
>
>   After 5 hours of the second day, the vision was born. Students would be charged with identifying a problem and using technology to solve the problem. We presented our concept that evening, even though there was mumbling and grumbling among some of the group until late into the night. By 10 p.m., we were still not finished with our presentation that we were to deliver the following day. Group members began losing their personal control, but the evening ended with much laughter at ourselves.
>
>   Thursday morning we presented our concept to the other teams and spent the rest of the day in planning with our own team. We had completed a framework with five themes and held a heavy discussion on assessment, which was not conclusive. We weren't surprised. On Friday, emotionally and mentally wrenched, having agreed, disagreed, and agreeing to disagree, we left the mountains feeling happy, sad, tired, but very much a team.

The Donegal team, with, as it turned out, limited support from their university partner, focused on empowering students to be agents of change. Each team of students was charged with the threefold task of identifying a problem relevant to their world, investigating the issue, and proposing a solution. The essential question students sought to answer was "What can I do to institute a change that will improve my school or community?" Identified areas of concern were close to home, in most cases in the middle school itself, issues such as cafeteria crowding, bus crowding and travel time, school vandalism and beautification, freedom of expression (e.g., dress codes), cafeteria food, and elective classes.

The teachers began with advice to the students: "Yes, you can arrange a meeting with the transportation director, but I am sure he has arranged the bus schedule the best way it can be run. And, certainly, your team can go ahead and talk to the food service director, but I know how hard she worked to arrange the lines for the most efficient service." Undeterred, the students worked out solutions to the problems, based on research using the computer lab, in a think-tank approach not unlike that which some industries use. They supported their cases with their findings, wrote their briefs, and arranged meetings with the transportation and food services directors.

As the students gathered information and created charts, graphs, and schedules, they prepared PowerPoint presentations to serve as documentation and as a report to the school board. Throughout the project, the students were found poring over bus schedules and routes, cafeteria menus and schedules—shoulder-to-shoulder with school personnel, including administrators.

Not only did the students successfully test their ideas, but school officials also implemented several of their recommendations. As a direct result of the students' work, more variety was added to the cafeteria menu; a new lunch bell schedule reduced overcrowding in the lunch lines; and new, more efficient bus routes were established.

INDIANA AREA SCHOOL DISTRICT / INDIANA UNIVERSITY OF PENNSYLVANIA

Sixth graders were in period clothing, vying to trade on the stock exchange in 1929, rushing from broker to broker, trading at high volume, watching the Dow Jones climb higher and higher. Then a voice came from the public

address box: "We have a disaster on our hands. The stock market has closed.
We do not know when it will reopen. The banks are also closing. We advise
you withdraw your money as soon as possible."

"I lost all my money," wailed a sixth-grade boy dressed in suit and tie. It
was only play money, but the look of disbelief on his face said it all. He was
completely involved in the 1929 stock market crash simulation—he was liv-
ing his own education.

Indiana Area School District is located in a pleasant college town geographically insular, the nearest city more than an hour's distance.
Substantial planning under the committed leadership of the director
of curriculum provided the basis for the project team leaders, who
then became the group leaders in their buildings. The only site in the
project to plan a program in one grade across all elementary buildings, Indiana looked first at content strands that would enhance the
students' study of genealogy, the industrial revolution, immigration,
and social movements. From building a human life-size replica of the
Statue of Liberty to experiencing a Depression-era soup kitchen, various simulations created a living history for students, parents, and
teachers.

By its own admission, the Indiana team felt quite confident that it
was a sound and solid team before arriving at the week's retreat. Although other teams were struggling with preliminaries already resolved by Indiana, by midweek the Indiana team was surprised to find
itself feeling tense and irritable: "We all wanted to talk at once; we all
wanted to remain silent at the same time. But we had to have a day
like this to understand the importance of working through problems
to make us a stronger, cohesive team." They also admitted that they
understood the mandate that a full team had to attend the 6-day Summer Training Institute:

> We had to encounter stumbling blocks to more fully appreciate that,
> when we got back to Indiana, we would be faced with bigger obstacles.
> We would have to sell this integrated curriculum to other sixth-grade
> teachers and specialists who had not been involved in the grant-writing
> and planning processes, as well as to four building principals who would
> be asked to provide the core team teachers with released time to evalu-
> ate and refine the curriculum once it was implemented. What got us
> through that day was a shared bag of M&Ms and meeting on the dance
> floor later that evening after dinner to dance to "YMCA" and to do the
> electric slide—together, as a group, once again.

Back home over the next few weeks, the team assembled all the materials they had accumulated and prepared a "you can't resist this one" presentation to the other sixth-grade teachers. Trusting in their professionalism and commitment to the project, the team plunged in, careful to be considerate leaders and not impose their ideas on those who had not attended the retreat. What made the difference between success and failure was the provision of released time for monthly meetings of the core team, subject teachers, and specialists to plan and build curriculum. Student teachers were included in the process and met with the teachers, helping to develop activities collaboratively.

The project provided the impetus for change at the university: The plan for a master's program, including thematic blocks rather than simple courses, began its way through the university senate. Furthermore, the school district indicated that this type of instruction did not add significantly to their budget. Most of the cost was in the form of releasing teachers from some other responsibilities to allow them time to work together on this project.

One of the most exciting simulations to occur at this site was the study of the 1920s and the stock market crash of 1929. Teachers began the scenario by giving the students "money," ostensibly as a reward for good behavior or good grades. After about a week, the children asked, "Why are we getting this money?" They were told, "Don't worry, good things are going to happen." Before long, students were walking around with this play money sticking out of their pockets.

The teachers then introduced the purpose and advantages of banking. The idea of interest on deposits was a natural lead-in to a discussion with the students as to how people accumulate excess money. After the students held a lot of money and understood the concept of interest, they wanted to earn even more on their investments. At that point the teachers introduced stocks and the stock market, posting the prices. Children began shouting, "Yes! Apple is up to 60!" They soon began making connections between the numbers of shares traded and the direction that the stock prices went. Some students even tried manipulating the market by encouraging their classmates to buy certain stocks, and they enjoyed watching the fluctuations in the market. Soon, students began selling off their stocks at high prices.

At about this time, a teacher from a different grade joined the scheme, creating bogus certificates and selling them. The following day, he walked into a classroom exclaiming, "I've got an idea for you. Forget about this stock market stuff. Buy bonds and they will double in value every day." The kids' eyes opened wide, and soon greed prevailed.

When the students returned the following day to pick up their doubled money, the teacher said, "Here, you bought one certificate, have another certificate. If you come back tomorrow with two certificates, I'll give you four certificates." The children did not yet comprehend that the wealth they were buying so cheaply and then accumulating was only on paper.

Later that week and without warning, the children heard over the public address system that the stock market had crashed. The announcer added, "Ivan Cougar, world renowned analyst, has left the country and investigations continue . . . more to follow on the six o'clock news." Ivan Cougar (played by the teacher selling certificates) had left the country with millions and millions of dollars in investors' money, leaving the bonds worthless.

In the classrooms, some children began crying because they had lost everything. After soothing the tears as best they could, teachers and student teachers, who with the students had been dressed in Roaring Twenties garb, somberly changed into Depression-era clothes to demonstrate sudden poverty to the students. Lunch that day was soup that had been weakened with water—served by the students' parents from a replica of the Depression-era soup kitchens.

MCNICHOLS PLAZA ELEMENTARY SCHOOL / UNIVERSITY OF SCRANTON

A school without walls . . . 13 different languages spoken at home . . . 22% of the students in English-as-a-second-language support . . . inner city. There was nothing going for this school except exceptional teachers with the creativity and determination to design and implement a vertical curriculum strand with arts as the core. Yet, instead of a despairing, depressing shaking of their heads or a look of defeat and anxiety in their eyes, there was a quickness to nod, to smile, to analyze and interpret a new idea or strategy or to share one that already worked, to improve upon a process, to celebrate.

McNichols Plaza is 1 of 13 elementary schools in a once-thriving city. The school is located in a part of the city with a high number of at-risk students. The building is an open-classroom facility, with no floor-to-ceiling walls, only classroom areas with abundant displays of student work throughout, from math concepts to visual arts. The Mc-Nichols team created an arts-driven environment for learning, managed collaboratively by the entire team of nine members. With a K–5 vertically stranded curriculum, the team focused on the cultural and ethnic diversity among its students.

McNichols's integrated curriculum project built on the school's grassroots restructuring efforts already in place and, particularly, on the efforts of a core group of teachers who had a long-standing routine of collaboratively planning their team-based lessons during their brown-bag lunch period. These teachers used the metaphor of seeds (students) and cultivators (teachers) for their concept of cultivating the children's success. Their story begins with a narration introducing the problem and then continues with an imaginary conversation among the supervising cultivators of the six pods, worried that the children (seeds) are not the way they used to be:

> Cultivators cared for and raised plants for both sustenance and beauty. Their careers were their work, and they had, until the last 5 or 6 years, felt great satisfaction from their work. It now seemed to take more work to get viable, sustainable plants, and it was difficult to discern precisely why some seeds came to them undernourished, unready to germinate. They asked themselves if they had produced inferior seeds in the past. Was it their fault, or were there other demographics at work that were out of their control? They looked at each other. The look deep in their eyes was disappointment, fear, anxiety, and confusion.

The team looked at what they had—personnel, facility, and other resources—and began their planning based on what could best help the children thrive.

> "You're not alone in this; I have the same problem in my quadrant: The seeds that do germinate just don't get their first leaves quickly, and their stems are weak. I put the lights directly over them—just like the book says. I talk and talk and talk to them, but they just don't respond."
>
> "I have these perfectly fine plans and perfectly fine plants. I open my book and check all the procedures—giving the proper tests at the proper intervals—everything just right. Then, before I know it, one plant is growing horizontally, one is doing a circular thing, one is leaning on another, and several seem to shrink instead of grow."
>
> "It's the preparation that the little seed has to undergo before it comes to us that I'm concerned about: the harvest, the careful packaging, the

climate control, the chemicals in the water supply—I'll swear there is something in the water—absorbed during the seed's formation."

Thus, these teachers began with a unifying theme of "Seeds, Seasons, and Celebrations," which centered on the universal commonality of the basic rhythms and cycles of nature: soil, seeds, plants, day, night, weather, and food. Their vision was to develop learners as members of the global community; blur the lines between teacher and learner; identify interconnections between people, art, and nature; address the needs of diverse learners; and explore and celebrate community cultural diversity.

If their seeds would not grow under the conditions to which they were traditionally accustomed, then the cultivators needed to find another way. There needed to be a change. In the succeeding weeks and months, they explored ways of growth that corresponded to the differences in seeds. Some needed to create uniquely beautiful textures, patterns, and shapes in characteristically arranged spaces. Most of these conformations were not usually accommodated within the confines of the standardized system.

The quadrant supervisors resolved to listen to each other, learn from each other, and seek out alternatives, and they soon rediscovered themselves as learners at their jobs. They found themselves with renewed energies that brought them to a meeting place in the mountains (the retreat) where others who were of the same mind gathered. It was there that a vision for their seeds was born and crystallized.

The McNichols project centered on the additional goal of identifying multiple perspectives reflected by the needs and interests of diverse individuals and ethnic communities within the larger school community. The team set its goals to guide students toward making connections between various sources of information from different subject areas, to identify instructional methods based on the needs of their diverse student population, and to investigate the diversity of cultures and individuals representative of the community.

CONNEAUT VALLEY HIGH SCHOOL / ALLEGHENY COLLEGE

No place to meet, no common planning time, no two team members with the same students, no telephone line for the new laptop computer provided by the project, intensive scheduling implemented without safeguards, various changes in building administration without notice, and band camp scheduled the same week as the mandatory Summer Training Institute for the project.

Conneaut Valley High School is a small school tucked into the northwest corner of the state near one of the Great Lakes. The site was selected for the project because of the zeal of an English teacher who has continually involved herself in professional development and opportunities that enrich the education of the school's students. Although it was evident from the first site visit that the teachers interested in an integrated curriculum had no administrative support, the representative from the Department of Education was touched by the dedication of the teachers who so wanted to develop a team, even in the face of adversity. All signs, except the team members and their sincerity, portended failure.

If ever a group of teachers deserved an opportunity to make a difference through collaboration and teaming, Conneaut Valley was it. Living in the shadow of a favored sister high school within the district, the Conneaut Valley teachers routinely were given no advance information regarding their teaching schedules, changes in building principal (three times within 1 year), and an intensive schedule being implemented without any teacher input.

By sheer will and devotion to their students, this group of teachers was determined to become a team that could collectively provide something enriching for their students. An English teacher, a technology teacher, a social studies teacher, a physics teacher, and the band director were forward thinkers and were looking for direction in planning and implementing an integrated unit designed to engage students in active learning.

As a number of Conneaut Valley teachers had been involved with Allegheny College's Center for Curricular Change, it seemed appropriate for the college to partner with the high school for this new project. In preparation, the teachers attended a weeklong summer session sponsored by the center, where they developed a number of goals and devised an action plan to carry out the project. With this, they felt ready for the Summer Training Institute. There was, however, one hitch: The institute was scheduled during one of the 2 weeks of the high school's band camp.

Although great latitude was offered for the curriculum content of the grant projects, one of the requirements was that a full team of eight educators (five from the school, three from the college) attend the Summer Institute in August. This attendance requirement was nonnegotiable, because the training in teaming was essential to the goals of the project. In the excitement of receiving the grant, the team had not realized the problem of band camp, but without the band director, a full team could not attend, and the opportunity provided by the grant would be lost.

When the director presented to his band the dilemma of the mandatory Summer Training Institute, scheduled the same week as band camp, he asked the students to weigh the good of the whole (the school, which would receive the grant) against the disruption of the scheduled band camp. Following a democratic discussion among the entire band membership without the presence of the director, a decision was reached: "Change band camp!" The students decided that the first week of the camp would go as scheduled; they would take a hiatus the next week while their director attended the institute, and camp would resume the following week. This decision confirmed the state project director's belief that the Conneaut Valley team could succeed.

That fall, after the institute, the teachers held their team meetings before and after school to discuss plans for the project. They held informal meetings between classes and at lunch to keep one another abreast of activities and progress. Their main form of communication, however, was in the form of memos, because the teachers did not see one another throughout the day. Thus, it was through cooperation and pure grit that the project succeeded. The teachers monitored project implementation and kept school district administrators informed, which was more than what they received in return. The administration ignored the project and would not acknowledge the need (and terms of agreement) for the teachers to have administrative support.

Early into the project, it became evident that there were few building operational procedures in place. The day that the gymnasium was needed for project demonstrations, the teachers had to strike a deal with the physical education teachers. (In fact, all of the teachers in the building had to fend for themselves.) There was no help given to the team in finding common space or a time to plan, and no attempt was made to schedule students interested in the project during a common class period. There was no place made available for a telephone connection for their laptop computer (donated to the school by the grant) to access the Internet. And no one—except the team and their students—seemed to care.

Student involvement in the Conneaut Valley project was based on the course schedules that students had for their senior year. They were chosen only if they had scheduled at least three of the following five classes: physics, English, sociology and social studies, computer science, and music (either choir or band). Interestingly, because the students were not together in one room at any given time, group work was completed by students on their own time. Thus, the time to build their musical instruments, write music and lyrics, and prepare a presentation took much longer than the originally planned 18 weeks.

Students created a number of unique musical instruments, including a calliope powered by a student-built air compressor system. They wrote melodies and lyrics and completed all required assignments related to their sociology, English, and physics courses. Because the content areas were interdependent, students were able to find connections among all five subject areas and incorporate those connections into their final projects. In their public performances, students had to play their instruments and incorporate a song with culturally significant lyrics. In addition, computer programs were created for the final exhibit before the performances presented on a Saturday evening to a full house.

SUMMARY

In a recent follow-up survey sent to the 10 schools that completed the project, 7 responded. Six of these 7 respondents are the sites. Results show that those sites considered most successful remain so even 10 years later, whereas the site that struggled has continued to face the same administrative problems that originally prevented the teachers from sustaining their work beyond the project. Even so, that site reported, "We are still a close group of colleagues," and it claimed that it was successful because of its enthusiasm, coupled with the training that the team members received. It cited students who "were in the program and [now] visit us, telling us they still fondly remember their experience" and question why it did not continue.

Those sites who have continued their teaming provide the following insights to the success and sustainability of their work:

- "We were successful because the team concept fulfilled a need for cohesiveness and coordination. Our team remained together because the concept of teams remained strong due to broad-based support. While only one of the original team members is still on a 'neighborhood team,' the teams are stronger than ever (10 years in existence, 3 years with original team)."

- "We are flexible and we are friends. We truly believe in what we do. Each year a 'guest teacher' becomes a member of the team for a year because our colleagues have seen that the core team is still enthusiastic (10 years with the same team)."
- "We remain a team because we have a purpose. We believe in the same thing, and we constantly challenge one another (10 years with the same team)."
- "We had a common commitment to acquiring new skills, sharing among ourselves. We realized that success was basically dependent upon us, not from being directed (10 years in existence, 9 years with the same team)."

The self-reported strengths of the team include the following most-cited comments:

- "The faculty believe in the value of teaming."
- "Teachers and principals understand the strength of sharing energy and expertise to make meaningful experiences that enliven the entire school culture."
- "Dedication of the core team, support of the administration, positive attitude of the students."

The top challenges faced today do not differ from those encountered at the inception of the project:

- "Scheduling common meeting times."
- "Dealing with a changing student population."
- "Having planning time."
- "Coping with district and state department of education restrictions."

Finally, the following are samples of the advice these teams give to others considering teaming:

- "Be prepared to make a sustained commitment."
- "Have broad-based support."

- "Be prepared to invest time and resources, including space for the team."
- "Build in common planning time."
- "Select teams whose members share a vision."
- "Be positive."
- "Be able to laugh."

Interestingly, these reflections are almost identical to the results of an evaluation conducted at the conclusion of the original project.

5

Taking One Step at a Time: Initiating and Implementing Team-Based Professional Development

Located atop a mountain in northeastern Pennsylvania, Mountain View Junior–Senior High School, like most rural school districts in the state, is nearly all Caucasian. Enrollment stands at 761 students. In many respects the district is comparable to small rural districts across Pennsylvania. In teacher commitment and creativity, along with administrative support, however, it is anything but average. In fact, it is just short of amazing.

"Culture Shock: Welcome to the County Where You Live" is not just a clever title for the humanities elective in Mountain View Junior–Senior High School. Rather, it is a philosophy designed by four teachers, all who wanted something more for their students and who intuitively sensed that their goal could best be accomplished by working as a team. The focus of the course—an elective—is the culture of Susquehanna County and includes history, geography, environment, government, business, art and architecture, literature, religion, tourism, and social activities. Its intent was, and remains, to provide students with the skills and knowledge necessary to carry out their work.

Included among the annual themes of the course are "Welcome to the Decade in Which You Live," "Effect of the Arts on Society," "The Millennium," "Women's Studies," "Mythology," "The Culture of Sports," "Etiquette," and in 1999 "Voices of War," which included a student initiative to design and build a monument honoring all veterans of the county. A fund-raising plan was launched, and 5 years later a stone monument was erected in front of the school. The culminating event was a dedication ceremony held in honor of the veterans of the county. The ceremony and reception were held on Veterans Day 2004 and featured service organizations as well as a dedicatory address by the graduate who spearheaded the effort.

Current students of Culture Shock continue to compliment the program as having made a difference in their lives and education in many ways. When asked how a team approach affected their learning in this class, students offered these and similar comments:

"[The teachers] work together to never let you fall behind."
"Expectations are high."
"Student input is welcomed."
"Someone could always answer our questions."

And, of course, there were many accolades about Culture Shock being their favorite course. Perhaps the most telling informal assessment was from Anne, who said, "This isn't just English or history; it is about the world. It takes us out of our own world." Probing questions led to the students noting that four teachers were in it together. Corey summarized, "They all knew all of us, and we couldn't pull anything. In fact, after about 2 weeks in the class, we didn't want to pull anything, because we saw teachers who really knew us and cared about us." The teachers attribute the success of the class to the dedication of a team. As a key member wrote,

> When we began, the concept of working as a team was a foreign concept to us. It turned out to be rewarding and liberating. . . . It forced me to rely on others; it made me listen and absorb; it taught me to compromise, and it helped me to express my thoughts and beliefs in a safe environment. [Teaming] has helped me grow both as a person and an educator over the past 10 years.

As testified by the teachers and shown by research, teaming can be transformational. The time that it takes is well worth the investment.

Lest it be thought by our emphasis on the teachers in the Keystone Integrated Framework Project sites that teachers are solely responsible for the success of team-based professional development, we think it is important to note that administrative leadership and support are primary to its success. The program simply does not happen without this commitment.

ROLE OF THE ADMINISTRATOR

If you are an administrator and are interested in a team-based process, you will be faced with three initial tasks: first, helping your faculty decide if and when they are ready for team-based professional development; second, conceptualizing the process, specifically, how it will best work in your building; and, third, setting up management procedures to ensure continued success. The unifying thread in all of these tasks is a belief in possibility. Team-based programs are almost always initiated by believers, who are usually, but not necessarily, the teachers. This is the optimal way to begin, but in reality an administrator needs to be both advocate and catalyst. Programs have a much better chance on initial approval and long-term survival if administrators pay close attention at the beginning to developing a working knowledge of the concept before beginning to promote it.

Because every school has a history of knowledge, beliefs, and assumptions about itself as an organization, an administrator can use these foundations to provide a beginning framework for team-based professional development. In addition, because the success of this initiative depends on stakeholders' beliefs about what is important in teaching and learning, these beliefs need to be acknowledged in the planning. Attention must be paid to "the way we do things around here," or there will be no support given by the traditionalists to changing the way of doing things. One effective way to approach change in the way that things are done is to identify and involve the school's unofficial historian—the person with whom everyone checks facts and dates of past events, as well as the values of the school.

Because the administrator—in this case, the principal—has a broader view of the institution than do the teachers, he or she can identify any earlier efforts tried or established with teaming. Team teaching itself is not new; thus, if the principal is new to the district, he or she may not be aware of past successes or roadblocks that his or her school may have experienced in teaming. No administrator wants to tout a great concept only to learn that something similar had been tried and had failed—not that previous failure should deter a school from a process that can improve the culture. Rather, the principal needs to know what pitfalls were encountered, and he or she needs to work with a team to address those pitfalls through the lens of this new approach, one that has the potential to result in positive ongoing systemic change.

The interest level of teachers, as well as that of the other administrators, is important to the success of the initiative. If there seems to be little interest because of a lack of understanding of the program, the principal can provide substantiated information to all potential stakeholders. Hence, she or he must be well informed and not just casually interested (unless she or he makes it clear at the outset that she or he is interested but needs to learn more about it). If the principal is well informed and can present that knowledge well, then even those who typically dislike any idea at first sight may at least listen to what the administrator has to say.

The principal should encourage the faculty to explore team-based professional development in the same manner as they have other school programs, by asking "What is it?" and "Will it benefit students?" If there are staff members with positive experiences in teaming, they can be asked to share their experiences with the faculty. Hearing colleagues talk about teaming experiences can stimulate interest. Sending staff members to visit sites that are successfully implementing this kind of professional development, or bringing people in from these schools to talk to faculty, can also get a fledgling idea off the ground.

After developing a working knowledge of team-based professional development, the principal should take the following steps to implement it.

Assess possibilities already in place. It is not necessary to reinvent the wheel. Instead, one should build on what is already in place. Enthusiasts as well as resisters will be more willing to expand what already works than to design a completely new program. Talk to a few faculty members who, you think, may be interested in further researching the topic, particularly, in gathering information on what colleagues have tried regarding any kind of teaming in the classroom or even in planning parallel or aligned curriculum. If there appears to be interest, introduce the concept to the entire faculty, beginning with a committee willing to take the time to research the concept and make a presentation to the full faculty. Some schools have already established committees who advise the principal on various staff development programs. If such is the case in your school, it is an ideal forum in which to discuss how to get the faculty to think about team-based professional development. We strongly suggest, however, that you begin slowly—with an invitation to persons who are interested and not with an administrative directive.

Determine existing resources and needs. Administrators generally assess needs and then find resources to meet those needs. With team-based professional development, it may be wiser to assess current and possible resources (such as the district's budget for professional development) and then decide what those resources can support (training, space, time, etc.). The district should also make a concerted effort to seek government grant funding, given that team-based professional development can be considered in the areas of school reform, teachers' professional development, and increasing student achievement. Use the team to brainstorm for what is unique about the school's particular program and use that as the hook for your proposal idea.

Gain support of stakeholders and decision makers. Without the support of all stakeholders and decision makers—the board, superintendent, curriculum director, professional development director, principal, teachers, parents—a successful program is not possible. The key to gaining that support is to involve all stakeholders and decision makers from the outset. Be aware not to overlook typical misperceptions and concerns. Each criticism must be countered:

"This is a frill and not needed."
"It may be all right, but it will cost too much money."
"Teachers should not be required to take this training."
"It will require more staff."
"Students will be confused."
"This is just one more thing on our plate."

. . . and so on. Rather, the principal can identify who is most likely to be interested in teaming, as well as a person who might serve as coordinator. Remember that a new initiative cannot be imposed; it must be a partnership among the district, the building, the principal, and the teachers.

Conceptualize the process. Administrators can help to structure initial conversations about team-based professional development by providing a framework for discussing the process. Such a framework helps those who plan the actual program and those who choose whether to fund it. There also is always the question of whether a particular program should be required. We favor giving teachers an option or providing a pilot program the first year with one or several teams. However, we suggest this favored option only if the school culture is comfortable with it. The principal and committee of teachers should make this decision together. The advantage of an optional or pilot program is that administrators and coordinators can start small and learn the ropes of managing this new concept. Another advantage is that all students who participate come with at least some motivation or interest and can help set a positive track record. Remember that the extent to which the team-based professional development program becomes institutionalized depends on its initial success, the culture of the school, and teachers' commitment.

Set up management procedures for success. Regardless of the design, administrators have to make decisions about the overall purpose and characteristics of the program. The program will have a longer life if the principal can articulate its purpose to the school board—particularly, the outcomes for students. The program should also be connected in clear terms with the school or district's mission statement, either of its goals, or both. Every school and district is different. Only programs that are carefully designed, implemented, and nurtured will last beyond a trial stage. Therefore, it is essential to keep records and submit reports on a regular basis (discussed in detail later).

Team-based professional development does not get off the ground without administrative guidance and championing of the cause. Programs that do get started without the principal can run into problems without someone to navigate past potential land mines—functions that principals are well equipped to handle. Administrators can play important roles that guarantee long-term success for team-based professional development, by asking the right questions initially, setting forth options and important choices, and developing management procedures.

ROLE OF TEACHERS

As shown by the research cited earlier and from the examples provided, teachers—like most other business and professional people—are effective and productive if they have a voice not only in planning their daily work but also in developing the overall framework for the jobs that they have been hired to do and, particularly, for the curriculum with which they are charged. Further, what we have experienced in our work with schools—and, especially, their involvement with professional development—is that teachers who are trained to work together, who are entrusted to make decisions, who are empowered to carry out the plan, and who are supported to do so express satisfaction, cooperate, and respect the changes that are being imposed on them. Administrators who understand this have the most success in initiating initiatives.

If you are a teacher interested in a team-based process, initiate a conversation with colleagues to see if they may be interested in further discussion. If so, meet with the principal to tell him or her that several of the faculty want to explore the idea of teaming in general and team-based professional development in particular. Make sure that you are prepared to answer initial questions that the principal might have. Ask if you can announce at a faculty meeting that interested teachers are being invited to form a focus group to explore the idea of team-based professional development and that this group will share the information with the entire faculty for further discussion. Assure everyone that this project is exploratory and that no decisions will be made by the focus group.

If appropriate, include in this group representative members from teams of teachers who have worked together successfully in some endeavor, not necessarily in team teaching. They can speak from experience and assure others in the group that, as a team, they learned to trust one another and the school officials. They can also attest that they had time to investigate, discuss, and analyze the possibilities of teaming; that they planned and implemented specific programs together; and that they had their questions and concerns listened to. These persons are likely to accept and champion new ideas because of their success in working in teams, and they can be valuable in bringing positive attitudes to the discussion. Of course, they will also be quick to relate any problems that they may have had.

Include the principal in this focus group. Some of the teachers may not like doing so, because they think that it prevents them from speaking freely, but you need the principal for the expertise and the authority that he or she can bring to take the idea forward. If the principal is one who has a tendency to take over meetings, then perhaps he or she can attend every other meeting and be offered reports about the other meetings. This pattern, although not optimal, can help allay the apprehension of the teachers as well as the principal, who rightfully needs to know what is happening in the building. Ideally, after several meetings, the teachers in the focus group will realize that it is important for the principal to be a working partner, because there must be support from the principal for the initiative to succeed.

If the focus group finds the concept of team-based professional development of greater interest as they learn more about it, they should prepare a list of talking points to review with the principal, and then they should present them to the entire faculty. Using the format of talking points is nonthreatening to the faculty members who are defensive about "what this focus group is going to tell us to do." Make sure that the person leading the discussion is comfortable in the role and that the entire focus group is prepared to answer questions. The principal should be invited to make comments. Remember that although not all members of the focus group may agree with every point, the group should be positive about the discussion with the entire faculty. What you want to gain from this faculty meeting is support for further discussion, a next step in the process.

This next step involves forming a working committee, which must include the principal. In all likelihood, the committee is self-selected and comprises those who are interested in teaming. This committee is centered on the details of logistics and works toward preparing a proposal to the faculty. This committee—or one led by the principal if this is a principal-led initiative—should carefully consider the constructs of teaming (addressed later).

As a note of caution, be aware that those who do not agree with the concept of team-based professional development may be holding their own informal meetings and possibly working to derail the plan. You know who these people are, if conversation stops when you enter the faculty room. It is wise to include one of these naysayers on the committee, even if you invite the person after the team is formed. The most important thing is that there is an open invitation for anyone to attend the committee meetings.

In the case of the Keystone project sites, some teachers had already formed informal teams who shared a common group of students or a common planning period, taught the same subject at different grade levels, or had similar views on teaching strategies. Teachers in other Keystone sites had been approached by a school administrator who asked them if they might be interested in a collaborative curriculum initiative. Yet another site had a teacher who convinced colleagues that teaming could be beneficial to teachers and students. Still another was initiated by higher education faculty members who approached teachers in the classrooms where they had placed student teachers, taking a chance that such teachers would be receptive to teaming. The important point is that teaming and a process of team-based professional development can originate in many ways from various sources.

INITIATION OF THE PROCESS

Although team-based professional development typically begins in schools that are engaged in or are preparing to engage in a new program, a school does not have to have a new initiative to introduce and develop team-based professional development. However, because team-based professional development is a process, it is best implemented in tandem with a new program initiative, such as integrated curriculum, literacy, attendance, curriculum standards, or any other similar schoolwide program. Building a team in isolation of a goal usually does not compare to the energy found in working on a project together. Many teachers recall professional development exercises that were carried out without their knowing the purpose. Do not make that mistake with the team-based professional process; rather, use this process to ensure that teachers can build a vested interest in team-based professional development, whatever the program initiative.

Research cited in previous chapters makes it clear that certain constructs need to be in place for effective professional growth and development of teachers. These include organizational support, professional responsibility of faculty, teaming, time, and communication. A school site that is considering implementing team-based professional development benefits from learning from these constructs and using the guidelines of this team-based professional development model while taking into account the culture of its institution. (Chapter 6 contains information on how to assess your readiness to proceed.)

As noted, it is best to begin with a willing team, one comprising teachers who are confident in their performance and have demonstrated success in the classroom. A team poised to be successful must have members that are committed to respecting one another's skills, points of view, and knowledge. The following sections discuss components within the constructs that make the difference between successful and unsuccessful sites.

It is important to take the time to address all of the following constructs in implementing and ensuring the sustainability of a team-based professional development program. None of these elements should be ignored, even if particular situations may not seem to warrant the time they take. All are essential for sustained success.

ORGANIZATIONAL SUPPORT

Even though a few teachers might form a group of colleagues to work as a team, without administrative support, team-based professional development will not become an integral part of the school culture. Both the district office administration and the building principal must support the idea, as well as the reality of team-based professional development, if it is to be initiated, implemented, and institutionalized. The administrators must believe that the process is good for the school, and they must be willing to be its advocate. The administration can also play a key role in identifying program priorities and providing input to establish clear objectives.

Creating Support

Principals play a central role in the success of team-based professional development by demonstrating their belief in and support of the process. For example, the principal can help initiate team-based professional development by doing the following:

- Becoming familiar with the underlying research
- Encouraging teachers to become familiar with the research and discuss the process among themselves
- Serving as liaison to the district administration, the school board, and the community
- Communicating with and garnering support from the district office
- Spending time with and giving advice to those willing to participate in team-based professional development
- Providing time for teachers to discuss and plan
- Designing a school schedule to accommodate plans developed by the teams

Even though the teacher committee prepares itself to answer questions as part of its presentation to the entire faculty, the principal must be conversant in this professional development model to respond to the inevitable questions and objections from teachers:

- "How is this better for me? for my students? for the district?"
- "What is the trade-off for the team planning period?"
- "Why do I have to teach with anyone?"
- "I don't want to plan my curriculum by committee."
- "Why do we have to do this?"
- "Where am I supposed to find the time to be part of a team?"

The principal must clearly support the belief that a team-based professional development process can pay dividends for a more successful school. And even if the school decides not to implement team-based professional development, this teaming yields an advantage to the principal in that it becomes an established process by which all other initiatives can have a high rate of success, because the teachers will have had the training to implement positive systemic change.

In a successful team-based professional development process, the principal becomes a full member of the team or meets with the team periodically to review its plans. The important element is that the principal be actively involved and openly supportive of the effort. If the principal cannot fully support the process, it has little chance of success. Because team-based professional development is a change in thinking, open communication and interaction among all members are essential to its success.

Faculty Support

Second only to principal commitment is the need to involve as many faculty members as possible. That is why forming a planning committee, as suggested, to report to the entire faculty is a good idea. Some schools choose to begin with a pilot program, training one team in the team-based process. However, the caution in this approach is that those not in the pilot program may become resentful; this can happen even if every teacher has been given the opportunity to be part of a team and receive training. Resentment usually arises not because persons want to be a part of a program but because those who are a part are perceived as receiving special treatment. That is why we recommend that the school or district include all faculty members in the discussions. If it decides to go forward with the training, it should offer the training to all who choose to be a part of the initiative. The skill required from the administration is neither to mandate nor to appear to discriminate against those who choose not to become a part of this model of professional development.

All teachers need to be informed at every stage of discussion, from faculty meetings to discussion sessions as part of in-service programs beginning a year before initiating team-based professional development. This planning helps to allay skepticism and negativism. And note that we are saying that it *helps* to allay, because every faculty group contains hard-line resisters, so planners should not expect willing buy-in from all teachers. Principals, therefore, should not coerce teachers to be part of a team; principals can only make it a positive experience to encourage teachers to be so.

All teachers must be given every opportunity to learn about the advantages to them individually as well as collectively. Administrators in one of the most successful sites in the Keystone project spent a year building commitment and developing a common philosophy while all the time empowering teachers to make changes. In less successful districts, a lack of commitment, empowerment, or common philosophy derailed the initiative.

Personal commitment on the part of the teachers is crucial for success, because it is clear that a chemistry needs to exist among team members. Teams with the most successful projects in studies of the Keystone framework were characterized by excellent cooperation and a confidence of collegiality. Team members got along well professionally and socially, and it was clear that they had contact with one another beyond the school day. The less successful teams, however, did not have much contact beyond normal school hours. In discussing the bond among team members, successful teams often noted that they always had good relationships among team members, but they thought that they would become closer and bond more now that they were in this new venture together.

District Office Support

The role of the superintendent is important, because the school community looks to the chief administrator to validate the planners' efforts. The superintendent can show support by doing the following:

- Encouraging the teachers to learn about team-based professional development and offering to meet with them

- Educating the school board in the advantages of, and voicing support for, team-based professional development.
- Inviting the teachers and principal to address the school board.
- Recommending board policy to support team-based professional development.
- Incorporating the goals of team-based professional development into district goals.
- Ensuring that appropriate public relations attention is given to the program.
- Providing support to the principal and communicating official endorsement of team-based professional development.

School Board Support

Although team-based professional development can be initiated by the administration or the teachers, it must have the support of the school board. The principal must seek approval from the superintendent for this professional development design and request permission to meet with the curriculum committee (or other appropriate committee) of the school board. Depending on the teachers' contract with the board, it may also be necessary to clear this design with the local teachers association. If that is the case, it is the teachers who should first approach their association representatives, if they are the ones initiating the design.

By meeting with the board committee, the principal can present the design and informally discuss the initiatives of the plan. Doing so provides a comfort level in which the board committee can ask questions and interact with the administrator out of public view, thus resolving any initial misconceptions, misgivings, and misunderstandings. More important, such a meeting ensures baseline support with the board committee as a stakeholder. Following this meeting and once the team of teachers has met and plans are formulated, the team and the principal should present their plan to the full board. Whether the presentation is in writing or in person, the proposal should be well prepared and based on research. A representative from the team needs to be available at the time the board takes action on the proposal, in case there are additional questions.

The school board's responsibility is to become familiar with the process of team-based professional development and to make informed decisions regarding its implementation, but all questions that individual board members are asked by their constituents should be referred to the superintendent or principal. The board must also commit resources if team-based professional development is to succeed. Before that commitment, however, the administration should carefully investigate the resources they already have and how these can best be utilized. It is possible that the team-based professional development will not require additional finances.

PROFESSIONAL RESPONSIBILITY

Professional responsibility for teachers means many things, both in and out of the classroom—for example, having the duty to care for students; exhibiting high standards of professional behavior and professional judgment; following school policy; providing research-based curriculum and assessment; conducting all activities with honesty and integrity; maintaining confidentiality; conducting oneself in such a manner as to protect and enhance the esteem and standing of public education; and undertaking appropriate ongoing professional development to promote competence in curriculum development, delivery and evaluation, classroom management, and teaching skills.

One of the unintended results of school districts' taking the responsibility for providing professional development through in-service days is that many teachers neglect to take any responsibility for their professional development, accepting whatever program districts provide. As professionals, teachers should take the initiative to seek ways to increase their knowledge and application of content and instructional strategies for the improvement of student learning. This commitment includes understanding student data and applying research to decision making in all aspects of teaching, including textbook selection, teaching methods, and assessment—all of which support instruction. Team-based professional development provides the opportunity for teachers to take responsibility in these areas.

Using Research to Support Instruction

An important belief of the team-based process is that research is the basis for data-driven decision making and for best practices in teaching. The implementation of the team-based process motivates teachers to read in depth and breadth the underlying premises for any instruction they might consider in their classrooms. What we found is that, with regularly scheduled team meetings, teachers realize the importance of using research-based information to support the recommendations that they are making concerning curriculum. Ideally, in a team situation, the result is based less on intuitive decision making, or what someone "just thinks is right," and more on decisions that are based on research.

The team-based model develops the capabilities of the team members to be innovative, work independently as well as collaboratively, set and solve problems, analyze critically, and handle large quantities of information from a range of media. These capabilities require the presence of a body of disciplinary knowledge, techniques used within a teaching discipline, and higher-order cognitive skills. Team-based professional development places a focus on this ability so that an entire team—and, preferably, the entire school—makes choices that are research based.

We wish to make clear, however, that this model is not designed to create pure academic researchers but rather to develop teachers' ability to conduct action research in their classrooms, as well as their capability to read and understand the underlying research of any proposed school program and to make meaning of it; to generate ideas applicable to teaching; to make decisions; and to reflect on the processes, including justifications for judgments and decisions. In summary, the team learns how to apply the research through thinking, discussion, planning, and reflection rather than simple reaction. In the early stages of team building, this use of research can be as basic as every team member's reading the same article, discussing it, using it (or deciding not to use it) as a basis for planning, and reflecting on the joint decision.

Teachers in the Keystone project who sought out the latest research had an understanding of why particular strategies worked and why others failed. The most successful teams were actively engaged in action research and were continually evaluating their teaching in light of current research in the field. It was clear that they kept up with reading professional journals and, as a result, understood and respected the theories that underlay their instruction.

TEAMING

A central office administrator succinctly characterized the teaming concept by saying, "What it boils down to is the ability of people to work and interact together as a collective unit." The importance of working together should not be underestimated, for with collective trust and collegiality, any program has a chance to succeed. Central to team-based professional development is, of course, team building. In general, team building uses effective communication and group process to address the specific conditions and constraints within the school and community. Through a group process, team members find that their success is tied to an overall effort in which everyone's involvement is valued. Each contribution builds on other contributions to result in large successes.

Although there are many definitions of a team, the following, by French and Bell (1995), aptly fits the purpose here: "A *team* is a small number of people with complimentary skills who are committed to a common purpose, set of performances goals, and approach for which they hold themselves mutually accountable" (p. 112). Larson and LaFasto (as cited in French and Bell, 1995), who studied high-performance groups, found eight characteristics that are always present:

1. A clear, elevating goal
2. A results-driven structure
3. Competent team members
4. Unified commitment
5. A collaborative climate
6. Standards of excellence
7. External support and recognition
8. Principled leadership

To be successful, a team must have a shared vision made up from the individual visions of team members. The shared vision of a team is developed from what each teacher (and the principal) sees regarding what the program should look like. Defining a shared vision from individual ones may take time, but it is important to take that time to do so, because it will become the "clear, elevating goal" that drives all other discussion and decisions.

The actual training should include information and perspectives on organizational systems, curriculum, and class schedules. Many teachers do not realize the importance of understanding systems and how so many factors enter into every decision in a building and school district, including scheduling. Because most of the misunderstandings between teachers and administrators on class assignments, curriculum, and scheduling are a result of not understanding one another's needs and perspectives, discussions of these areas need to take place early in the training so that there is a common understanding and focus on systemic and organizational structure. For example, principals often view scheduling as sacrosanct and may appear to be unyielding to any suggestions that schedules, curriculum, and class assignments possibly can be improved. However, a benefit of the collaboration between administration and teachers is the opportunity for the teacher teams to help design a schedule that can be flexible to their needs without disrupting the schedules of colleagues. This flexible approach makes it possible for the teacher teams to combine classes and extend time for particular course work. It also reflects a high level of professionalism (i.e., being responsible to meet district requirements). As a result, a stronger collaboration can be developed between the team and the principal. More important, it is the shared vision and the understanding and utilization of these systems that lead the process of successful team building. Other necessary elements for successful team building include the following 10 requirements, from individuals and from the team as a whole:

1. The team must set clear expectations and identify the anticipated outcomes.
2. Each member needs to understand why he or she is on the team. Even if the team members are self-selected, they all need to be clear in their own minds as to why they are there to be part of the team.
3. Team members need to be committed to the project—or, initially, to exploring the project.
4. Team members need to feel that everyone is competent and that everyone has the resources, strategies, and support to fulfill the tasks.
5. The team needs to define the timeline to accomplish its tasks.
6. The team has the freedom and empowerment needed to accomplish its goals. Team members need to understand the team's accountability process and the limits of their authority.
7. The team needs to understand team and group processes. Roles and responsibilities of each member need to be defined. Team members need to learn the skills of problem solving, process, goal setting, and measurement of results. They also need to establish rules of conduct in areas such as conflict resolution, consensus decision making, and carrying out action plans.

8. Team members need to be clear about the priority of their tasks and communicate clearly and honestly with each other.
9. The team needs to feel support from the organization, and it needs to be coordinated by administrative leadership that assists it in obtaining what is needed for success.
10. Team members need to feel valued for their service and see rewards in their achieving positive change.

All of these elements should be reviewed in the initial team meeting, and assurances must be provided by the administration that assistance or facilitation will be provided to aid the team in discussion of these elements and how they will lead to shared understanding of the team's work and common goal.

It is important to secure early involvement of everyone who might be affected by or become interested in the initiative. Further, it is vital to ensure shared decision making about general issues, such as conception and implementation, as well as more specific issues, such as teacher assignments, student placement, curriculum, and scheduling within the program or project. For example, for team-based professional development to be effective, the team members should share the same students so that their learning styles, intelligences, personalities, work styles, and achievement levels can all be part of planning the appropriate instructional strategies.

For purposes of enriching the curriculum content, it is best to have a framework based on a theme, a unit, a standard, or an objective—any of which helps the team organize and collaborate toward a product. With the No Child Left Behind mandate and with curriculum content being driven by national and state standards, teams working to design and align curriculum to meet such standards can be the best solution that a district can support to help all students succeed.

Teachers find that working together in planning curriculum and units to meet standards is much more effective than working in isolation. Everyone's strengths bring a richer result in the content and instructional strategies. Where possible, team teaching should be a part of these strategies, and opportunities for teaching together in the same room should also be part of the planning. Teaching together provides the opportunity to interact with one another's teaching style and subject knowledge, thus enriching the delivery of instruction. It also allows for teachers to view the same students under the same conditions, rather than discuss student work in the typical frame of reference, such as "Stan in my class does one thing" and "Stan in your class does another."

Where possible, the instructional strategies should evolve into an integrated curriculum, which is not only more manageable than numerous individual curricula but also a pedagogically sound element of school reform. A synthesized, integrated curriculum based on research and developed over time through collaborative efforts is much more powerful than one designed and delivered by an individual. Shared ownership of the curriculum leads to frequent updates when research leads the planning.

Once team collaboration is established through writing the curriculum, a common plan for assessment of the students' work is essential. This plan leads to students and teachers who know the expectations and the measurement of those expectations, and it leads to the team's conveying the resulting assessment to students and parents. The objective here is to develop a strong team that has common students so that all efforts are concentrated on content, instructional strategies, and assessments that are based on research and targeted toward the students shared by the team.

More important, it is necessary to advocate flexibility in accepting all points of view and adaptability in using existing strengths and challenges of individuals and resources related to the project. That is, successful implementation is not necessarily a function of ideal conditions or resources. Rather, teams need to consider what people and resources are available, what is possible to supplement through further training or materials, and what challenges to the program or project need to be accepted as constraints within which to operate.

TIME

Ask any teacher what is most needed to do a better job, and the first response is always "more time." Time was the most important item identified by the Keystone project team members as being a necessary element for success. Even in discussing the issue of money resources, participants said that money was important only in that it could buy time.

In American schools, teachers have traditionally been expected to find their own time to develop and update their knowledge and skills to maximize student learning. This is not the case in European and

Japanese schools nor in American corporations, all of which provide company time for employees to improve their knowledge and skills. If American schools are to become high-performing learning enterprises, they must rearrange their schedules to make better use of existing time for teachers to learn and keep abreast of change (Renyi, 1996). Common planning time—time to meet and work together—is particularly essential for a successful collaborative program or project. This is one reason why it is so important to have administrative support to arrange for this needed time. Ideally, all team members should have a common planning time every day if they are team teaching and at least a semiweekly planning time if they are developing a project or program.

Districts may need to be creative regarding how they can arrange for common planning time, such as through extended lunch periods for the team, additional staff, or extending the day (with compensation). One Keystone site hired a substitute for part of each day so that the music teacher (a member of the team) could attend the team planning period. Team members at another site met during their lunch period (not ideal, but doable). Resourceful administrators and the teams should be able to work together to resolve this time issue, and, perhaps through their efforts, all teachers will benefit, with the ultimate beneficiary being the students, who will gain through the increased knowledge and skills of their teachers.

Although schools' contracts and cultures are different from one another and the issue of time needs to be addressed individually, schools are encouraged to be resourceful and inventive. For instance, local business and industry personnel often get corporate credit for volunteering in schools. The principal or superintendent should meet with these groups—perhaps through the area chamber of commerce or local business association—to discuss the possibility of persons coming in to cover duties such as teaching or monitoring lunch or study periods so that teams can meet. Retired teachers are another untapped resource in most communities; asking these persons to volunteer their time would take care of any certification issues. Many of these retirees already volunteer as tutors or readers in elementary schools, and it is likely that they or colleagues are willing to help cover classes so that the team members can have a common planning time. Some districts offer tax credits to senior citizens who give time to the schools. It is worth looking into these possibilities and perhaps generating even more ideas for solutions.

COMMUNICATION

Nearly every survey of any business or organization reveals the importance of good communication. Communication is the major activity and the most important component engaged in by school administrators and, by association, the most important component engaged in by all groups and programs supported by administrators.

Keeping records from the beginning of the initiative and establishing a filing system makes the process of team-based professional development manageable. A project planner is helpful, as is the sample planning forms included in this book (see chapter 6). Minutes should be kept of every meeting—include attendees, agenda items, action taken, and who is responsible for what.

Communication in the form of reports is particularly important, because these reports become the record of work. Make sure to provide periodic reports to the superintendent through the principal and to faculty who may not yet be part of a team. These reports should be strictly informational and should not be used as an avenue for debate, confrontations, or lobbying.

As the team-based professional development progresses, periodic written reports should be made to the board. These reports keep the board informed so that the team and the board are insured against unexpected challenges by interest groups. It is always good practice to keep all stakeholders informed, particularly, the governing body of the institution.

Students of the teachers participating in this professional development model should ultimately make presentations to the board. These students can demonstrate skills learned in the classroom as a direct result of the instructional strategies that the teachers learned through the team-based professional development process.

There are several ways to communicate to others the progress and success of your team's work. One technique is to e-mail all other teachers in the building on a regular basis, such as the beginning, middle, or end of each month. The team should decide on a consistent style, such as one using bullet points, a letter format, questions and answers, points of information, or benchmarks. If one of the team members is particularly skilled in writing and volunteers to be the communicator, he or she may do so as long as all team members have input and the opportunity to review the communication before sending it.

An important element of clear communication is appropriate language style. Although this detail may seem to be frivolous, it is not. We have all learned that careless informal communication, such as that sometimes used in e-mail, can be misinterpreted, and we have all misunderstood something that someone has said to us in passing or in haste. That is why all communication, written or oral, should be reviewed as to the impact that it might have on the receiver. Any time that written communication is to be shared with others, it should first be read as if one were the receiver seeing it for the first time.

The following directives should help guide your written information:

- Use simple, direct sentences.
- Write short paragraphs.
- Be factual and specific, highlighting the specifics by placing them at the beginning (ideal) or end of sentences and paragraphs.
- Be positive. Use words that convey an upbeat attitude.
- Set off important material by bulleting, but do not overuse lists.
- Do not lead with bad news and do not place blame.
- Proofread (both print and electronic communication).
- Tailor the information to the audience.

It is also wise to have in place a system for responding to questions that any reader may have.

Being publicly recognized in a positive light is important in professional development. Therefore, using positive public relations as part of a team-based professional development model is important in that it formalizes a process of connecting to the public and builds a relationship with the media. Thus, guidelines for local media should be developed by the teacher teams, such as the following:

- Decide collaboratively what should be publicized.
- Draft the text, emphasizing the most important elements.
- Provide high-quality photos with identification where applicable, electronically if requested.
- Request coverage by the media for major events.
- Write thank-you messages from the team.
- Credit the media in reports that the team makes to the school board.

Another way to provide positive information and further educate colleagues is through a *media blitz*, which can be as simple as sending one- or two-page summaries of research articles pertaining to the program being implemented by the team and offering to send the entire article (or its web address, if online) to any reader. These communiqués can be sent (placed in in-house mailboxes) monthly or bimonthly to be effective but should be published on a regular schedule. In time, some of the media blitz documents may be original articles written by team members, rather than summaries of already-published articles. Media blitz articles should also be sent to the superintendent, with enough copies for the school board. It is at the discretion of the superintendent whether to include these in the board packets. The team should not be upset if the documents are not always distributed. Another possible system of communication is the use of a webpage, best placed on the district's website. A newsletter is another possibility, and it is a good idea to send such a newsletter to parents, perhaps once each semester. The important thing to remember is that there are many ways to send a message, limited only by the team's imagination.

A PLACE OF ONE'S OWN

We want to to add a sixth construct as being desirable, if not necessary. A team functions best if it has its own space. It is good organizational practice to have a designated area for any activity and, particularly, for one that requires people to meet and access materials. Meetings that are held in a designated location for common planning time increases productivity and aids in their beginning promptly. A common space is also important in sustaining a professional process. If teams are scurrying around looking for a place to meet, time will be wasted, and team members will be concentrating more on finding where they should be rather than on what they are doing.

To maintain the atmosphere that the team is a working group and not just a means for the teachers to gain free time, the space should be large enough to contain a table, around which all of the members can be seated comfortably. In addition to the table and chairs, several carrels or desks should be included so that team members can use this area during their personal planning period as well. A chalkboard or flip chart is also desirable, and a designated computer is a must. Because paper, books, and materials accumulate and sources from the Internet are accessed, storage space, including a filing cabinet and shelves, is needed in this common location. If a complete room is not available, at least an area of a classroom, library, media resource room, or the like should be made available to the team.

Conducting business in a designated space adds weight to all planning and is the best place to post the team's action plan as a daily reminder of the work to be done (information on developing action plans can be found in chapter 6). During meetings, all members of the team should share their various instructional strategies, discussing what they have used since the previous meeting, what worked and why, and what plans they have for any changes. It is important to establish this routine of input from all team members, because it acknowledges the team concept and enriches the discussion. Each team member should also keep a log or journal of all discussions, to serve as a reflective record of decisions reached and as a potential resource for later designs of instructional strategies or possible publication.

Team space is important because the team members should be conducting collaborative research following training in research design and techniques, if needed. Space shared by the team members leads to collaboration in the research, first as primary discussion, then in integrating the findings. The designated computer allows for the research to proceed without interruption. This access does not preclude research at a university library, but on-site access to information expedites and encourages not only more research but also additional collaboration, because the team members are based at the same site in conducting their research interests.

What is most valued in having a specified area for the team is the recognition that its work is a professional activity and is an excellent way to validate the process of team-based professional development. The aforementioned suggestions emphasize and remind all stakeholders of the professionalism of the team. Additionally, presentations at professional conferences provide an appropriate outlet for teachers to showcase their accomplishments and contribute to the body of professional literature in their fields.

6

How Do You Know It's Working? Organizing and Monitoring Professional Development Programs

Today, teachers are barraged with demands from parents, administrators, state and federal agencies, legislators, and other public and private organizations to be accountable for student learning and the billions of dollars spent on education. At the national level, standardized tests—along with state and federal assessments (particularly, those in mathematics and reading)—have become the most visible measures of how schools are performing. Tremendous resources at the state and federal levels have been directed at measuring successes and failures through testing of student learning. Unfortunately, far fewer resources are allocated to professional development aimed at improving all aspects of schooling, fewer still to determining if it has a positive impact on teaching and learning. A model of professional development that is cyclical and self-evaluating makes more efficient use of precious resources.

Team-based professional development is a holistic approach to professional development where teachers take control over their learning and development. It is a multifaceted approach to professional development with an emphasis on process and change. Thus, the evaluation of team-based professional development must likewise be multifaceted. Determining the attitudes, skills, and behaviors needed to improve teaching and learning across multiple grade and subject levels, documenting changes, and justifying the effort can seem like a daunting task, but taken one step at a time, it can provide valuable information about the efficacy of the effort.

This chapter is written for all involved to read but is directed primarily toward those who want to monitor their progress toward effective teaching and learning. Evaluating professional development is a cyclical rather than a linear process—that is, there is no end point that signals completion. Instead, new information is constantly collected and considered, resulting in modifications to ongoing action plans. The following sections will guide you through resources that help start the evaluation process. Provided here are types of data that are useful in establishing goals and objectives—examples of how to assess teachers' concerns and attitudes, organize action plans, and monitor the effectiveness of your professional development efforts. The information provided is not a rigid blueprint to evaluate all professional development; rather, it provides you with a place to start, and it illustrates the kinds of information important to building and maintaining your team-based professional development plan.

ANALYZE DATA

A good place to start is to analyze as much data as possible. Data analysis should include an array of measures. Examine student achievement data from local, state, and national tests. Examine district data collected on students, such as attendance patterns, disciplinary actions, participation in extracurricular and cocurricular activities. Class grades and teacher assessments of student strengths and weaknesses can also be useful. In short, examine all data that you can get your hands on, to form a broad image of the current status of student learning in your school.

District- and class-level aggregate scores are what is most often reported. Be sure to drill down, however, and take a look at the data in as many ways as possible. For example, although reading scores on standardized tests might indicate that the district is doing fairly well, ask yourself, are there specific grade levels or certain skills that need improving? For example, vocabulary scores on a reading test might be in an acceptable range, but perhaps reading comprehension scores are low. Further, they may be lower for a particular subgroup (e.g., one based on gender, race and ethnicity, socioeconomics). Be sure to explore where the differences lie, and focus your efforts toward improving those; that is, target areas of greatest need.

To be sure, available data do not provide a complete and thorough map of the greatest opportunities for improvement. Rather, such analyses provide the basis for productive discussions about your school or district and help to keep the discussions on track. Look for gaps between where you want teaching and learning to be and where they currently are. If average daily attendance is low and you think it productive to focus on increasing it, setting reasonable targets will help you on your way. Examine your instructional practices honestly, and try to identify areas in which you might need some assistance to improve your own performance. Elementary teachers, for example, often cite a lack of science content in the curriculum as a reason for not teaching science more. Secondary teachers typically have little foundation in teaching reading and are at a loss for helping students read and comprehend better. Be honest, take stock, and develop a plan.

Carefully examine the district curriculum and assessments. Making sure that they focus on state and national standards and that they direct all efforts toward attaining district goals and strategic planning priorities sets everyone on a common path. Consider the way in which progress down that path is assessed. Identify whether it accurately addresses issues important to the district.

ESTABLISH GOALS AND OBJECTIVES

The importance of clear goals and well-defined objectives cannot be understated. As Thomas Guskey (1997) stated,

> It has been suggested that the reason Moses spent 40 years wandering in the desert is that he didn't have an operational definition of "The Promised Land." The same could be said for many of our efforts in professional development. We wander aimlessly without a clear idea of what we want to accomplish or how to measure our progress. (p. 3)

An important distinction must be made between goals and objectives. Goals are broad statements that focus on overall intent. Objectives, however, are specific statements that are typically measurable and observable. Goals are where you want to be; objectives are the specific steps that you take to get there. President John F. Kennedy's famous speech in May 1961 stated "that this nation should commit itself to achieving the goal, before this decade is out, of landing a man on the moon and returning him safely to the earth." Kennedy's statement set the goal. How we got there was the result of an infinite number of smaller steps (objectives) all leading in the same direction. Although the world could likely have gotten along without space ice cream, the entire goal would have faltered without achieving the objectives of developing reliable rocket and heat-shield technologies.

Discussions about student achievement, teaching practices, curriculum, and assessment are important, and it is likely that many issues will rise to the surface. You must decide where you want to be in 6 months, 1 year, 3 years, and so on. Only by determining your destination can you plan the trip. For example, you might want to improve your class's reading scores (goal) by increasing students' recreational reading time, helping students select appropriate reading materials, and creating an atmosphere that values reading (objectives). Each objective should be stated in a form that includes whom the objective is aimed at (audience), what behavior is desired (behavior), how the student will be expected to accomplish it (condition), and what criteria must be met (degree). Audience, behavior, condition, and degree are sometimes called the *ABCDs* of objectives. Using the example, a properly stated objective that helps to achieve the goal might be the following: "Given the opportunity to choose their own reading material and a quiet time during the school day, students will increase the amount of time they spend actively reading in a 30-minute period as measured by the teacher's systematic observation of time on task." Set your goals, achieve your objectives, find the promised land, and land your astronaut on the moon.

A word of caution, however; do not try to solve all the problems at once. Focus primarily on those that are achievable in the beginning, and tackle the more daunting problems as you make progress. Think of the Swiss cheese theory—if you continually nibble small holes in the weaknesses, they disappear and allow you to start nibbling at the larger issues. Develop a track record of success, and more success will follow.

ASSESS TEACHER CONCERNS

Remember that almost no one likes change. It is usually an uncomfortable process that requires looking closely at your beliefs, motivation, and practices, along with an admission that you just might need some improvement. Consider that, regardless of what you do, changes happen, so why not put yourself in charge of the change by using evaluation tools that can help the change process?

The concerns-based adoption model provides one framework to begin the process, and it is based on more than 35 years of research (e.g., Fuller, 1969; Hall, George, & Rutherford, 1979; Hall & Hord, 1987, 2006). *Concerns-based* means simply that for change to occur, the concerns of all involved must be identified and addressed. Horsley and Loucks-Horsley (1998) stated that the concerns-based adoption model has proven itself an indispensable tool for developing and continually evaluating reform efforts, because it addresses concerns that most people have when facing change. If you consider that you have already made a major change by becoming involved in a whole new way of thinking about professional development, then you will soon realize that using these assessments should not be seen as a threat. Actually, they will probably help make your case even stronger for using team-based professional development. If you have made a professional statement by choosing team-based professional development, now support that choice.

The concerns-based adoption model addresses seven stages of concern reflecting attitudes about proposed change—awareness, information, personal, management, consequence, collaboration, and refocusing (Hall & Hord, 2006). Our current interest is in identifying teacher concerns, which, according to the model, involve the following:

1. Awareness—little concern or involvement
2. Information—general awareness and interest in learning more
3. Personal—uncertainty about the demands and ability to meet them
4. Management—attention on the processes and tasks
5. Consequence—impact on students
6. Collaboration—coordination and cooperation with others
7. Refocusing—exploring benefits and possibility of major changes

The Stages of Concern Questionnaire is a 35-item survey instrument that requests a response on a 7-point Likert scale (see Figure 6.1). Responses indicate the intensity of the concern about each statement. The response options range from 0 (*irrelevant*) to 7 (*very true of me now*). Directions for respondents are provided with the instrument.

Name: _____

Date completed: _____

It is very important for continuity in processing this data that we have a unique number that you can remember. Please use:

Last four digits of your Social Security number: _____ _____ _____ _____

The purpose of this questionnaire is to determine what people who are using or thinking about using various programs are concerned about at various times during the innovation adoption process. The items were developed from typical responses of school and college teachers who ranged from no knowledge at all about various programs to many years experience in using them. Therefore, *a good part of the items on this questionnaire may appear to be of little relevance or irrelevant to you at this time.* For the completely irrelevant items, please circle "0" on the scale. Other items will represent those concerns you *do* have, in varying degrees of intensity, and should be marked higher on the scale, according to the explanation at the top of each of the following pages.

For example:

This statement is very true of me at this time.	0	1	2	3	4	5	6	(7)
This statement is somewhat true of me now.	0	1	2	3	(4)	5	6	7
This statement is not at all true of me at this time.	0	(1)	2	3	4	5	6	7
This statement is irrelevant to me.	(0)	1	2	3	4	5	6	7

Please respond to the items in terms of *your present concerns*, or how you feel about your involvement or potential involvement with _____. We do not hold to any one definition of this program, so please think of it in terms of *your own perceptions* of what it involves. Since this questionnaire is used for a variety of innovations, the name _____ never appears. However, phrases such as "the innovation," "this approach," and "the new system" all refer to _____. Remember to respond to each item in terms of your present concerns about your involvement or potential involvement with _____.

Thank you for taking the time to complete this task.

1. I am concerned about students' attitudes toward this innovation.	0	1	2	3	4	5	6	7
2. I now know of some other approaches that might work better.	0	1	2	3	4	5	6	7
3. I don't even know what the innovation is.	0	1	2	3	4	5	6	7

(*continued*)

Figure 6.1. Stages of Concern Questionnaire

4. I am concerned about not having enough time to organize myself each day.	0	1	2	3	4	5	6	7
5. I would like to help other faculty in their use of the innovation.	0	1	2	3	4	5	6	7
6. I have a very limited knowledge about the innovation.	0	1	2	3	4	5	6	7
7. I would like to know the effect of this reorganization on my professional status.	0	1	2	3	4	5	6	7
8. I am concerned about conflict between my interests and my responsibilities.	0	1	2	3	4	5	6	7
9. I am concerned about revising my use of the innovation.	0	1	2	3	4	5	6	7
10. I would like to develop working relationships with both our faculty and outside faculty using this innovation.	0	1	2	3	4	5	6	7
11. I am concerned about how the innovation affects students.	0	1	2	3	4	5	6	7
12. I am concerned about this innovation.	0	1	2	3	4	5	6	7
13. I would like to know who will make the decisions in the new system.	0	1	2	3	4	5	6	7
14. I would like to discuss the possibility of using the innovation.	0	1	2	3	4	5	6	7
15. I would like to know what resources are available if we decide to adopt this innovation.	0	1	2	3	4	5	6	7
16. I am concerned about my inability to manage all the innovation requires.	0	1	2	3	4	5	6	7
17. I would like to know how my teaching or administration is supposed to change.	0	1	2	3	4	5	6	7
18. I would like to familiarize other departments or persons with the progress of this new approach.	0	1	2	3	4	5	6	7
19. I am concerned about evaluating my impact on students.	0	1	2	3	4	5	6	7
20. I would like to revise the innovation's instructional approach.	0	1	2	3	4	5	6	7
21. I am completely occupied with other things.	0	1	2	3	4	5	6	7

22. I would like to modify our use of the innovation based on the experiences of our students.	0	1	2	3	4	5	6	7
23. Although I don't know about this innovation, I am concerned about other things in the area.	0	1	2	3	4	5	6	7
24. I would like to excite my students about their part in this approach.	0	1	2	3	4	5	6	7
25. I am concerned about my time spent working with nonacademic problems related to this innovation.	0	1	2	3	4	5	6	7
26. I would like to know what the use of the innovation will require in the immediate future.	0	1	2	3	4	5	6	7
27. I would like to coordinate my efforts with others to maximize the innovation's effects.	0	1	2	3	4	5	6	7
28. I would like to have more information on time and energy commitments required by this innovation.	0	1	2	3	4	5	6	7
29. I would like to know what other faculty are doing in this area.	0	1	2	3	4	5	6	7
30. At this time, I am not interested in learning about the innovation.	0	1	2	3	4	5	6	7
31. I would like to determine how to supplement, enhance, or replace the innovation.	0	1	2	3	4	5	6	7
32. I would like to use feedback from students to change the program.	0	1	2	3	4	5	6	7
33. I would like to know how my role will change when I am using the innovation.	0	1	2	3	4	5	6	7
34. Coordination of tasks and people is taking too much of my time.	0	1	2	3	4	5	6	7
35. I would like to know how this innovation is better than what we have now.	0	1	2	3	4	5	6	7

Please complete the following:

36. What other concerns, if any, do you have at this time? (Please describe them using complete sentences.)

(continued)

> 37. Briefly describe your job function.
>
>
>
> For scoring instructions and interpretation, see Hall and Hord (2006). Reprinted with permission of the authors.

To ensure useful results, teachers must understand exactly what they are to do, have sufficient time to complete all items, and respond honestly and thoughtfully. All responses are anonymous, and administrators must take careful and obvious steps to ensure anonymity. Areas of greatest concern can be addressed as you proceed in implementing team-based professional development.

PROFESSIONAL DEVELOPMENT INVENTORY

The Professional Development Inventory (PDI; Melnick & Witmer, 1999) was developed to determine differences between highly successful and less successful sites participating in a statewide project that involved teachers working in teams (see Figure 6.2). The PDI consists of 38 items used to assess teachers' perceptions of the five areas thought to be essential to success in team-based professional development: communication, organizational support, professional responsibility, teamwork, and time. The PDI can be used as a preassessment and a periodic reassessment to determine progress.

The PDI asks teachers to indicate how strongly they agree or disagree with each statement, using a 5-point scale. The information yielded by this scale can be used to provide a snapshot of the climate for successful professional development before a team launches any new initiative. The following directions explain what teachers are to do.

Scoring of the PDI is done to determine overall perceptions of communication, organizational support, professional responsibility, teamwork, and time to identify areas that may need special attention in your action plan. Scoring is best done for the whole group so that individuals can feel free to answer all questions honestly. To score the PDI, the following point values are used for each response on the PDI scoring sheet (*strongly agree* = 5; *agree* = 4; *undecided* = 3; *disagree* = 2;

Instructions: The following statements are related to several different aspects of teaching. This survey is intended to determine your perceptions and provide guidance to professional development planners. Please address the items on this survey in terms of your current professional position. The items address a wide range of issues considered to be essential to good teaching and collaboration. Think in terms of the team of teachers you work with daily.

Please rate each statement according to the following scale by circling the appropriate response.

Strongly Disagree = SD
Disagree = D
Undecided = U
Agree = A
Strongly Agree = SA

1. We keep all constituencies informed of new initiatives.	SD	D	U	A	SA
2. Our teachers work well together.	SD	D	U	A	SA
3. My district supports me in attending conferences and training sessions.	SD	D	U	A	SA
4. We use student assessment data to improve our own instruction.	SD	D	U	A	SA
5. I have the time to discuss important issues with colleagues.	SD	D	U	A	SA
6. Administration asks my preference of teaching assignments.	SD	D	U	A	SA
7. I respect my colleagues.	SD	D	U	A	SA
8. I have planning time each day.	SD	D	U	A	SA
9. We can alter the daily schedule to meet our teaching needs.	SD	D	U	A	SA
10. My colleagues and I notify the newspaper of school activities.	SD	D	U	A	SA
11. My colleagues and I make adjustments in our teaching based on student performance.	SD	D	U	A	SA
12. The district provides in-service time to issues we have identified.	SD	D	U	A	SA
13. I make presentations to my colleagues about curriculum or teaching innovations.	SD	D	U	A	SA
14. There is a sense of common purpose among teachers I work with.	SD	D	U	A	SA

(*continued*)

Figure 6.2. Professional Development Inventory

15.	Other teachers and I meet together to discuss instructional strategies.	SD	D	U	A	SA
16.	My colleagues and I work together to find research to guide and support our teaching.	SD	D	U	A	SA
17.	The teachers have in-service time to meet for team planning.	SD	D	U	A	SA
18.	I team-teach with at least one other teacher.	SD	D	U	A	SA
19.	My building principal encourages professional growth.	SD	D	U	A	SA
20.	Other teachers and I work together to develop new materials.	SD	D	U	A	SA
21.	My colleagues and I collaboratively plan professional development activities.	SD	D	U	A	SA
22.	I send home frequent news bulletins about things in my classroom.	SD	D	U	A	SA
23.	I feel a professional responsibility to tell others about successful teaching strategies.	SD	D	U	A	SA
24.	We develop plans for improvement.	SD	D	U	A	SA
25.	The school board supports new initiatives.	SD	D	U	A	SA
26.	I have input into the choice of professional library materials.	SD	D	U	A	SA
27.	The administration builds the schedule based on our instructional needs.	SD	D	U	A	SA
28.	My administrator finds ways to provide the resources we need.	SD	D	U	A	SA
29.	We find time every day to discuss instruction.	SD	D	U	A	SA
30.	Teachers work together to improve instruction.	SD	D	U	A	SA
31.	Teachers I work with help me choose instructional materials that support our teaching.	SD	D	U	A	SA
32.	My colleagues exhibit a high degree of professionalism.	SD	D	U	A	SA
33.	My colleagues and I identify our own professional development needs.	SD	D	U	A	SA
34.	We keep the administration well informed about our program.	SD	D	U	A	SA
35.	The school district provides in-service programs relevant to our instructional needs.	SD	D	U	A	SA
36.	I have time to meet during the school day with my colleagues to plan and reflect.	SD	D	U	A	SA
37.	The district has provided a professional library containing books and journals for my use.	SD	D	U	A	SA
38.	I like the other people on my team.	SD	D	U	A	SA

SCALE SCORING SHEET

Scoring key:
5 = Strongly agree (SA)
4 = Agree (A)
3 = Undecided (U)
2 = Disagree (D)
1 = Strongly disagree (SD)

Communication	Organizational Support	Professional Responsibility	Teamwork	Time
1. _____	3. _____	23. _____	2. _____	5. _____
10. _____	6. _____	24. _____	4. _____	15. _____
22. _____	8. _____	32. _____	7. _____	29. _____
34. _____	9. _____	33. _____	11. _____	36. _____
	12. _____		13. _____	
	17. _____		14. _____	
	19. _____		16. _____	
	25. _____		18. _____	
	26. _____		20. _____	
	27. _____		21. _____	
	28. _____		30. _____	
	35. _____		31. _____	
	37. _____		38. _____	

RAW SCORE

_____	_____	_____	_____	_____
of 20	of 65	of 20	of 65	of 20

SCORE INTERPRETATION

	Communication	Organizational Support	Professional Responsibility	Teamwork	Time
High	15+	48+	17+	53+	15+
Average	13	44	16	48	12
Low	11	38	14	44	9

strongly disagree = 1). Add each column to obtain a raw score for each of the five areas. This is best done with a spreadsheet (e.g., Excel) or with statistical software (e.g., SPSS), particularly when there are large numbers of respondents.

Each scale is interpreted in relation to its total possible score. The PDI scoring sheet provides complete instructions and should be interpreted accordingly, using the high, average, and low designations on the scoring sheet. By doing so, evaluators and team members get a fairly good picture of the perceived strengths and weaknesses of the school and district.

ACTION PLAN

The action plan is a simple tool that organizes all facets of team-based professional development and keeps track of each aspect of the project (see Figure 6.3). Using this simple tool, anyone can become a master organizer. The team needs to monitor the goals, objectives, and activities associated with each objective; who is responsible for seeing that activities are accomplished; what financial and human resources are required to complete the activity; and what the target dates are for completion, without spending large amounts of time managing the

---

_____
(School name)
1. Goal:_____
2. Objective:_____
3. Evaluation of the objective:_____

4. Activities:	5. Persons responsible:	6. Schedule:	8. Evidence of accomplishment:

Summary evaluation assessment:
_____ Achieved beyond expectations
_____ Achieved
_____ Partially achieved
_____ Not achieved

Note: One action plan page is completed for each objective.

Figure 6.3.   Keystone Integrated Framework Project, Action Plan

information. Our action plan form is a simple way to plan the project and monitor its progress.

Each goal might require several action plan sheets, each of which lists one objective per page. For each objective, list the activities required to accomplish it, who is responsible to see that each activity is completed, when the activity will be started and finished, and what evidence is acceptable to conclude that the activity has been completed. By completing these action plan forms at the beginning of each new initiative, your team can plan, manage, track, and evaluate its progress toward accomplishing its goals.

So far, you have analyzed data, decided where you want to go, planned how you need to get there, and organized your effort. Follow your action plan to the promised land. These steps focus your efforts on productive activities and help you achieve your goals and objectives.

7

What If It Happens? Institutionalizing and Sustaining Team-Based Professional Development

"I know it sounds strange, but for the first time in my professional career I feel like I am in charge of my own destiny and the future of the students. It is so heartening to be able to plan the content and activities as a team of teachers who trust one another and who have built a trusting relationship through which we can openly discuss our plans. I don't feel challenged by my team members probing questions about the lesson, but rather I know I am supported with suggestions to improve, expand, or enhance my lessons."

"As an art teacher, I've never felt part of the group. The teachers in the buildings where I travel see me as relief—someone who gives them a break. It's always been clear they think I merely keep the kids busy while they plan the real lessons children must learn. It's been frustrating and demeaning as a professional. This project, however, has injected and instilled new life into me. It has reinvigorated my career. For the first time—and I've been teaching for more than 20 years—I'm being included in planning sessions with other teachers, and I feel like a member of the team. My contributions are valued, and the content of my art classes now complement what the children do in their regular classrooms."

"I have never worked so hard in my life, nor have I ever felt so strongly that what I do actually matters."

"I could never go back to the way we were before team-based professional development. I like my team and have built strong professional and social ties with them. It may sound corny, but with a team behind me I feel empowered."

"Despite our diversity of personality, educational expertise, teaching style, and, in some cases, philosophy, we are a team, and that has made all the difference."

WHERE DO WE GO FROM HERE?

For years, many good teachers had only the role model of the Little Red Hen to follow. They identified with her as she sought assistance in the task of making bread—from planting the seeds, watering the soil, harvesting the wheat, going to the mill, preparing the dough, and baking the bread—only to be rebuffed by each of the other farm animals. Had she had the help of the others in the barnyard, as well as the support of the chicken farmer, she would not have had to do all of the work required to produce a loaf of bread. Many good teachers find that they—like the Little Red Hen—have had to do it all. True, there is a certain satisfaction to saying to the laggards, "Then I will water the seeds" and "Then I will bake the bread," but it is nothing like the personal and shared satisfaction that a team-based effort can produce.

WORKING AS A TEAM

The paradigm shift from isolation to team-based efforts leads to a kind of thinking and acting that becomes the way that one teaches and behaves as a professional educator. The shift further leads to a form of self-discovery, a process provided only by working together, time, and reflection. Ultimately, successful team-based professional development is the confidence that comes from sharing success among members of the team. It is the validation of peers who understand what the individual team member is achieving, as well as what they as a team are accomplishing collectively.

Once your team has reached the point of working as a unit, you have reached the third of four stages of group development, a longtime popular process developed by Tuckman (1965) and still used today. The four stages include the following:

Stage 1: Forming—when a group is just learning to deal with one another, a time when minimal work is accomplished. At this stage the individual roles and responsibilities are unclear. The added interest in team-based professional development is that, while Tuckman says that the leader must be prepared to answer a lot of questions, in a team-based model the leader is not always evident and certainly not appointed initially; if anything, the leader emerges.

Stage 2: Storming—a time of stressful negotiation of the terms under which the team will work together. At this point team members may vie for position as they establish themselves in relation to other team members. This is why having a clear purpose defined at the outset is very important so as not to let emotions rule.

Stage 3: Norming—a time in which roles are accepted, team feeling develops, and information is freely shared. At this stage roles are more clearly defined by the team members, but major decisions are made by the entire team. This is also a good time to engage in social activities with the team—discussed in detail later.

Stage 4: Performing—when optimal levels are realized—in productivity, quality, decision making, allocation of resources, and interpersonal interdependence. At this point the team clearly knows why it is doing what it is doing and focuses on the shared vision.

By now, the team should have a high degree of autonomy, and although disagreements occur, they are being resolved within the team, whose members agree to any needed changes in processes and structure. Most important, at this stage the team members look out for one another.

Indicators that your team has reached the final stage, performing (institutionalization), include the five conditions identified by Nolan (quoted in Siens & Ebmeier, 1996) as those necessary to facilitate changes in teacher thinking and behavior:

1. "focused, descriptive records of actual teaching and learning events,"

2. "development of a supportive relationship,"
3. "continuity over time,"
4. "teacher [team] management," and
5. "reflection by both [teacher and administrator]" (p. 317).

Note that these five factors include the terms that have formed a recurring theme throughout this book: *support, time, keeping records, teacher empowerment,* and *reflection.* None of these can be taken for granted, and each must be continually worked on. It is the intent of the information in this chapter to help your team institutionalize the process that you have developed to build team-based professional development and any programming that accompanied that professional development.

RECORDS

Keeping records is foremost for institutionalizing and sustainability. Change always brings detractors, and your team needs to have records as evidence of the meetings held and the work produced. Records include reports to the principal and superintendent; newsletters to all constituents; teacher-written articles and reflections; and presentations to other teachers, students, parents, administrators, board members. Other records to keep are assessments that demonstrate student progress, student perception, and teacher satisfaction. We also suggest that you establish a webpage that can be accessed through your school district's website. Assign one of your team members to post reports for the superintendent, newsletters, articles that your team members have written, curriculum, and links to research that supports team-based professional development and the programs that your team is offering. Where possible, organize your records using the action plans in chapter 6; it helps you to manage the information and provide a way of documenting progress.

SUPPORT

Keeping records is important for reports that your team will make to the superintendent and the school board and for newsletters to faculty and parents. It is by keeping all stakeholders well informed that support can be sustained. A process for responding to questions is also important. Do not ever assume that "everything is fine." If you are lax in keeping records, you may be defenseless upon questioning. If you cannot show progress, you may not be making any, and it is likely that you will lose support.

Like people in any relationship, team members need to work on supporting their relationships with one another. That support needs to be nurtured. Teachers likely begin the teaming development with trust in one another; they now need to work to hold and increase that trust.

Agree among yourselves that you will not speak ill of any team member and that you will resolve any differences within the confines of the team. Regardless of the differences—and there will be differences of opinion—present a united front as a team and make all team responses in agreement. Think about your school's administrative team. Rarely, if ever, will you hear any member openly criticize an administrative colleague. Standing together gives them collective power and can do the same for your team.

PLAN SOCIAL EVENTS

You do not have to be one another's best friends outside of school, but periodically having dinner together or attending a conference or a 1-day planning retreat as a team is highly recommended. Social events can include spouses and other faculty if the events are not used as decision-making occasions. In other words, do not talk shop unless only the team members are part of the event.

TIME

The precious commodity of time cannot be overemphasized because it provides evidence of how you use your time and it shows that time for the team is essential. Time provides the all-important opportunity for supportive feedback by team members, and it decreases isolation.

Keeping a log of the time that all members of the team spend on their program shows how the team utilizes this resource in research, planning, development, writing, and—most of all—teaching. As a team, you must also spend your time well, which means that you are to use time designated for team planning for only that purpose—that is, for planning. Even if you are "running errands" for the team project, consider the impression that your leaving the building is making. It is difficult to make a case for the necessity of team planning time if that time is not used for that express purpose.

TEAM MANAGEMENT

Teacher management is at the heart of team-based professional development, and those on the team must strive to maintain the team approach and devise and implement ways to do so, in addition to the support addressed earlier.

Hold regularly scheduled meetings. Continually set goals and diligently follow the guidelines provided in the forms in chapter 6, particularly, the action plan format, which makes team management *manageable*. On task lists, write the names of those responsible for each task. Clearly define roles and responsibilities. Compliment one another on successes. Support one another. Offer help when a team member is struggling. (Further suggestions are offered in the section on sustaining the change.)

REFLECTION

Reflection is the element most easily neglected by teams, because time for reflection must be scheduled and a conscientious effort must be made to focus oral and written deliberations on the work and results of the team. Reflection allows for teachers to think about their teaching and its effects on student achievement. Reflection also provides a needed process to think about one's personal satisfaction and how it affects teaching. If the individual team members are uncomfortable taking the time to reflect on their attitudes, then schedule time to reflect as a group and use the white board. Reflection is not a frill; it is a necessary step in the planning and sustaining process, and it is a factor in high-level job performance.

PITFALLS AND HURDLES

No matter how well organized your process and how smooth your journey, you will experience pitfalls and hurdles. As with any new program or process, the path will not be smooth, having various impediments for teams to overcome for continued success. Each team at any given site finds different challenges, and not every possible barrier can be foreseen. However, by planning for these potential problems, you can prepare to cope with them in a positive matter.

Your team needs to discuss potential barriers and develop a plan to address concerns. The key is to approach hindrances objectively, not personally. Assign specific challenges to designated responders according to their specialties. This action goes a long way in a team's being prepared with options and responses. Identify the problems, analyze and discuss them, and look at various solutions. Few problems are ever totally unsolvable. It is time well spent toward sustainability.

Naysayers

Every organization has its share of naysayers and faultfinders. Such negative people try to ruin even the best attempts at any change. They can cast a shadow on an otherwise sunny culture, trying to erode efforts to improve. Approximately 15% of people in any organization are negative; 10% are positive; and 75% are somewhere in the middle, the undecided majority who first reflect on a given situation before they decide to react negatively or positively (Witmer, 2006). This middle group is the one that must be convinced: Its members usually do not act until a position is clear to them. Addressing this middle 75% is the best method of neutralizing the poison of the negative 15%. The undecided 75% therefore needs to be kept informed with accurate positive information.

Roadblocks

There will be roadblocks, whether they are colleagues, a board member, a vocal parent, funding, or even a team member's teaching schedule or reassignment that seems to prevent that person from joining team meetings. Team members need to discuss roadblocks in advance so that when a situation occurs, team members remember not to comment individually until all of the members can meet, discuss, and strategize.

Not all roadblocks will be intentional, but the team needs to discuss any barrier to implementation. The team must focus on a response or solution to the roadblock by first determining if it is a major deterrent or just a nuisance (see section on criticism). Next, the group needs to discuss the origin and the potential impact. Anger and frustration should be kept within the walls of the meeting space. Perhaps the roadblock will not be viewed as such by the person who put it in place, or its impact may not be as strong as the team first thought. It is also possible that what appears to be a roadblock will become an opportunity to find options and a better alternative.

Regardless of the kind of hindrance, the team must develop a strategy to overcome it. The team members need to make lists and be clear in their plan to address the impediment. This may be as simple as taking the problem and the team's recommended solution to the principal. If this is a situation concerning the principal or is a problem that is more complicated, then the team needs to devise a menu of possible solutions. No one should assume that the principal will automatically solve the problem. The solution needs to be a team effort. In some cases, someone other than the principal might be the best person to take the action; in other situations, all team members may be actively involved. Whatever the response, it needs to be a joint effort, and team members need to carefully review all consequences before taking any action.

Team Disagreements

There will be many times when team members do not agree among themselves. The best way to come to resolution in these disagreements is to use a white board, flip chart, or SMART Board (a large, interactive, touch-sensitive white board that connects to a computer) to make lists. From the lists, the group can determine the issues of difference and the points of agreement. Clarifying the issues often resolves them. If not, then the team should make more lists, adding and deleting items as the discussion becomes focused. If a resolution does not become clear, then the team members need to clarify what they are in agreement with and what still needs to be resolved. They should make no major decisions until all points have been discussed and everyone has had a voice. Voting can be divisive, so it is better to come back to the discussion than to end it by a vote. Keep the disagreement about issues; do not let it become personal.

Criticism

Be prepared for criticism. There will be those who do not agree with what you are doing. It may be that they are uncomfortable with change or that they philosophically disagree with team-based professional development. More than likely, however, they are just expressing displeasure with the attention that your team is receiving, or they may perceive that you are being shown favoritism. There is a mentality in most organizations that if one group receives what looks like special privileges, then it must mean that something is being taken from another group—namely, that of the person holding the negative thought. Be prepared for this attitude, even in schools in which everyone has an equal opportunity to participate in the team-based professional development process.

Criticism may come from colleagues or parents. The usual areas of criticism include lack of rigor in the program, student assessment, class scheduling, teaching assignments, parents' skepticism, nonagreement of the goals, perception that goals are not being met, and teachers association issues.

One can respond to criticism in several ways. One approach is to ignore it. A second is to seek out the source of the criticism and speak directly to that person or persons. A third way is to discuss the criticism with the principal, not to ask or expect him or her to handle the issue, but to ask if he or she is aware of the comments and to indicate which approach your team plans to take to address the critics. This discussion may give you insight into how serious the criticism is. A fourth approach is to address the criticism in your reports or newsletters. Thorough and ongoing communication with all constituencies is an effective deterrent to unwarranted criticism.

A fifth approach is to call a meeting to discuss the criticism. The team should discuss all rumors and evidence of criticism and determine which of five tactics to take in each instance:

1. Ignoring criticism is the easiest, but it may be interpreted as evidence that the critics were correct. However, if the criticism is minor, sometimes ignoring it is the best way.
2. Seeking out the source of the criticism is a good technique because it shows confidence on the part of the team and can demonstrate concern that others may be misunderstanding the work of the team. Never confront the alleged source of the criti-

cism. Rather, ask the person if two members of the team can meet with him or her. Do not be defensive and do not show anger. The purpose of the meeting is to resolve misconceptions. If the person with whom the team members are meeting becomes defensive and denies having criticized, ask who the originator is, because the team would like to discuss the situation with that person. The team members then need to decide how far they want to investigate the criticism.

3. Do not meet with the principal to deliver a problem for her or him to solve. Approach the meeting as one to share concerns with her or him as a member of the team. Because it is your problem, you are there to gather information and to seek advice—if the principal offers it. Make sure that you have a solution or two in mind before taking the problem to any administrator, and never appear as if you are tattling.

4. By the time that the team is in the performing stage and poised to institutionalize team-based professional development, it will have had the opportunity to see the value of reports to the principal and superintendent, as well as that of all newsletters to constituents. These early and consistent information streams establish your credibility and provide a recognized forum for addressing issues related to the work of the team. Be sure to use the tone that has been consistent in these documents, which is to inform the reader and not to defend your actions.

5. Calling a meeting to address criticisms is the least recommended way to respond to critics, because it risks making the team members vulnerable in an open forum, with the possibility of their not being able to objectively explain their work. If, however, a criticism is so potentially harmful that it threatens the team's work, use an external, trained, and experienced facilitator. Otherwise, positions on all sides stand a good chance of becoming personal attacks.

SUSTAINING THE CHANGE

One of the most difficult and often overlooked steps in any change process is acknowledging that change requires maintenance as well as planning for expansion. If your team recognizes and accepts that it is typical at times to feel stagnant or discouraged, you will be better prepared to address this natural development state and turn it into a positive progression.

Once you have had some success and gained some confidence, it should be easier to expand, refine the process, take some chances, make some changes, and take time to relax and celebrate.

Revisiting the Goals

Sometimes circumstances change, and you need to adjust or change the original goals. Plan to review goals at least once a year or after an event that might affect your goals and mission. Having conducted some of the surveys and assessments suggested in chapter 6 should provide direction for your discussion. Few of us ever think to revisit goals in an individual classroom, but now that you are part of a team, it is important to talk about the results of your work in light of your future as a team.

An annual planning retreat is the best time to revisit the goals, because you will have time to create your new action plan in light of those new goals. Begin by a review of the current goals, what evidence you have to show that you met them, and to what extent. Do not drop a goal only because you have not achieved it. Make sure that any goal that is removed is done so because it is no longer relevant to the mission. Also, do not remove a goal without replacing it with another (unless your original list of goals is too long and unrealistic).

Once new goals have been identified, make a poster, preferably done commercially or in the school's graphic shop or printing office and sturdy enough and large enough to be posted in the team meeting room or the space where you meet. Make smaller sizes to place on the desk of each team member. More important, do not forget to share these goal changes on your website, reports to the administration, and newsletters.

Checking State and District Policies

State policies that affect the work that you are doing sometimes change without your being aware of them. However, because state education policies also affect school district policies, it is wise to review that document annually. The principal should have a copy of the school district's board policy manual; if not, then the team should request a copy from the superintendent. If it is not forthcoming, then arrange to hold a team meeting at the district office so that the team can collectively review the policy manual. Just to set everyone's mind at ease, explain your reason for wanting to review the manual, and ask if the school board secretary can flag all new policies that have changed during the past year.

If you go to the district office to read the policy manual, it might be an opportunity to meet briefly (ask for half an hour) with the superintendent to bring him or her up to date with your work and your future plans. This is simply a face-to-face information meeting, not a time to ask for personal favors. If you have questions that only the superintendent can answer, then submit an agenda with those questions a week in advance of the meeting and ask if the superintendent is willing to address those questions (making sure you have copied the document to the principal). Also make sure that your questions are specific to the work of the team and team-based professional development. This is not the time to discuss any other issues. The more professional your approach, the more attention the administrator will pay your team.

Networking With Other School Sites

Meeting with teams in other school sites is a positive step to take. It provides opportunities to share missions, goals, successes, failures, future plans, and common concerns—such as meeting space, time, scheduling, curriculum, and—of course—team-based professional development techniques. If you have not yet partnered with another school who is using team-based professional development, make it a point in your team's annual goal revisiting to identify another school and contact its team. A meeting with teachers and administrators who are using team-based professional development adds a dimension to your outlook and planning for the future.

One of the most limiting aspects of teaching is the lack of networking, so take any chance that you can to meet educators from another school site. Even if you do not immediately see an advantage to meeting others who are experiencing team-based professional development, a year from now you will wonder why you never thought of it before. Remember teacher isolation? Here is another way to create not only connections for your team members but also possibilities for other teachers in your school to establish contacts with peers in other school sites.

Expanding the Area of Participation

If there are a limited number of teams at your school site, now is the time to expand the team-based professional development involvement. Offer an after-school meeting or part of an in-service day to speak informally to others in your school district who might be interested in teaming. An informal face-to-face meeting is an effective way to recruit others who may be more interested than they were when the original team-based professional development program was offered.

You can begin by providing an overview (no more than 5–8 minutes) in which each team member talks about one aspect of team-based professional development and how it has changed him or her. A good technique involves having a list of questions prepared in advance, questions that your team thinks the attendees might want to ask, or you might prepare a list of talking points based on questions that you initially had or ones that colleagues have asked you in the past. Use these lists if there is an initial hesitancy for the attendees to start asking questions, or simply have them on the table with headings such as "What you may have wondered about what we do," "Things you may want to know but didn't want to ask," "So you don't want to work in a team," or "Ten good reasons why team-based professional development could work for you." Use your imagination based on the experiences in your school site.

Be honest and thorough in your responses to the questions, and have examples of results with you—student projects or student comments, parent reactions, changes in student attendance, decreases in discipline problems, or increases in student achievement. Provide suggestions for how interested colleagues can become a part of team-based professional development or obtain more information. It helps to have the principal join the meeting at a designated time or be part of the entire meeting, depending on her or his involvement and the role that she or he plays in the team. It is also best to have a moderator who can keep the pace moving but not be in charge of the meeting. The team members assume that leadership role.

Expanding Communication

Expanding communication can be achieved in a number of ways, including the recruiting meeting just described. Your team can prepare a newsletter for faculty at a different building level than that of the original team. In addition, you can request to meet with faculties throughout the district. For example, if you are a high school team, do a 20-minute presentation to the middle school and elementary school faculties.

Prepare newspaper articles, and invite the media to observe your team meetings and teaching, if you are using team teaching or doing something about which they could base a news article or television clip. Ask to be interviewed by the local radio and television stations, by sending them a brief description of who you are and why you are teaming. Describing an anecdote from a classroom situation is a good way to get their attention—but make sure it is attention grabbing in a positive way. Success stories of how kids turned around from not doing well to becoming engaged is always of interest, so tell such a story without mentioning names and tie that success to the positive effect of team-based professional development. Another way to get the media's attention is to emphasize that you are adapting corporate techniques for school teams. The media is typically interested in new ways that teachers do business.

Invite parents to visit the classrooms of the teachers on the team, preferably, during the school day, when the students can demonstrate the results of the team-based professional development of their teachers. Prepare a brochure or single-sheet handout giving a brief description of how teaming positively affects the teachers and their teaching, and then let the lesson demonstrate how the input of several teachers can enrich any given class. Perhaps a demonstration of how teachers brainstorm ideas that positively affect the students can be a part of the presentation, although this technique works well during an evening open house, when students may not be available to be part of a demonstration lesson.

It is now time to make a presentation to the school board. Ask for 10 minutes on the agenda, and do the presentation live, leaving documentation in writing for the board members to review later. Discuss with the superintendent whether to invite questions from the board members. The superintendent should then alert the board in advance of the type of presentation to expect from the team.

If your team has not yet had direct contact with the university that typically serves your area, it is appropriate at this stage to connect with their department, school, or college of education to discuss mutual interests and concerns, particularly if the university has a teacher preparation program or a master's-level program in education. There may also be shared research interests and opportunities for partnerships for study or grant funding for further team-based professional development projects.

Dealing With Changes in the Membership of the Team

Although there have not been published studies in the teacher retention rate of those who are engaged in team-based professional development, we would not be surprised if such studies showed that teachers who are involved in teaming—particularly, in team-based professional development—have a higher retention rate than that of teachers who remain in educational isolation. In one case, we know of a teacher who delayed his retirement for 2 years because he was having too much fun. Based on (a) our belief and experience that team-based professional development provides a camaraderie and positive work environment not otherwise possible and (b) related research, such as a survey of superintendents from the North Central Regional Educational Laboratory on teacher retention (Hare & Heap, 2001a), it is likely that teacher retention rates are different for team-based professional development participants. The laboratory's conclusions stated that "three lower-cost strategies that improve the professionalism of teaching were rated as effective or more effective than strategies such as increasing teacher salaries [in retaining teachers]. These strategies are *involving teachers in decision-making, implementing team or interdisciplinary teaching, and making scheduling changes to allow common planning time for teachers.*"

A study on Delaware's Tech Prep program revealed that teachers experience less isolation and burnout when they team up to create integrated, interdisciplinary teams (Academic Innovations, n.d.). There is also research on the retention of new teachers that will likely be the basis for needed research on the retention rate of teachers in team-based professional development programs, because many of the elements are the same. Through a study on new teacher retention, Wong and Wong (2003) stated,

> Because new teachers want to be part of a team and part of a culture, the focus of induction is on training. The major role of the trainers is to immerse new teachers in the district's culture and to unite them with everyone in the district as a cohesive, supportive instructional team. . . . *What keeps good teachers are structured, sustained, intensive professional development programs* that allow new teachers to observe others, to be ob-

served by others, and to be part of networks or study groups where all teachers share together, grow together, and learn to respect each other's work.

Even with higher retention rates of teachers who team, a team will face changes in its membership through teacher retirement, relocation, reassignment, career change or advancement, death, or a team's falling out. As with most changes, those anticipated are easier to deal with than those that are unexpected.

Anticipated changes of the team composition can be planned with time for the team to recruit colleagues who have expressed interest. If the team also team teaches, however, the selection of a replacement team member may be complicated if a teacher of a particular discipline at the grade level needed is not interested or if the new person hired is not interested in team-based professional development. Here is one of the many instances in which having the principal on the team is helpful. If the principal is engaged with the team, then he or she is more likely to recognize the importance of finding a replacement who will be a good match. In the best scenario, members of the team are invited to be part of the recruitment process, and the expectations of teaming are made clear to the candidates for the position.

In the case of an unexpected vacancy, the emotional reaction will vary, depending on the circumstance of the vacancy. It is important for the remaining team members to meet as soon as possible following the vacancy to mourn and regroup. A substitute will likely be assigned to fill the teaching vacancy; that person should be supported if he or she will be team teaching with the team members, but that person should not be expected, unless through his or her choice, to be part of the team policy planning. It is prudent of the principal to meet with the team before the arrival of the substitute—and again after his or her arrival—so that all parties understand their roles.

In all cases, a change in the composition of the team affects the working of the team and the team-based professional development. Patience and support are required of all involved. If possible, one of the existing team members should volunteer to mentor the new team member; doing so makes the change easier for everyone.

Preparing for Stress—Team or Individual

Team stress can occur at any time, even in the midst of success. Remember, this is a whole new environment for most of you. Even though one of the negatives of working alone was that you did not have another adult to talk to, now that you are part of a team, you may be longing to be by yourself and not have to interact with peers. Before teaming, you could generally arrange the order in which you offered particular lessons, and if you wanted to do composition on Tuesdays and Thursdays, you could. No one challenged the content that you presented, except the occasional administrator who wanted to let you know that his or her minor was in your discipline.

Now, you find yourself as part of a group that is developing curriculum and perhaps arranging the schedule. Whereas you once approached your discipline sequentially, you may now be doing it thematically so that the disciplines of the team align. Also, negotiating with the team members sometimes takes more time and effort than what any of you had anticipated. It is enough to drive all of you crazy some days. The team stress might include differences of philosophy among the members, but perhaps the worst stress might be the negative reactions of people not on the team from whom you would least expect it. However, closing ranks among the team members and getting through those confrontations makes your team stronger. All in all, you will likely find yourselves saying, "We wouldn't change this and go back to the way it was for anything."

In the meantime, stress is real, and you can use three basic strategies to deal with it. You can alter your environment, avoid the situation, or accept it.

1. To alter your environment is to first understand that you cannot change other people. Too often we say, "If only so-and-so would . . ." You cannot force anyone do anything, so you need to change your own behavior. Express to others how you feel, but do not keep saying that someone else "should" do this or that. Instead, try saying, "I need," "I want to," "I'm going to." This strategy can work with teammates as well as those outside the group who may be confronting the group.

2. There are times when it is better to avoid the situation by just walking away from it. Come back to the problem when you have the time and patience to deal with it. When you are angry or upset and you know that your coping skills are at ebb, try going for a walk. Remember to tell someone on the team that you just need to get away for a little while and that no one should take it personally.

3. When you can do nothing to alter or avoid the situation, you may just have to accept it., You must first, however, discuss it with the team. Try to find a solution through the discussion, but if the situation cannot be altered, you will only increase your own stress and that of the group by belaboring it. In such cases, you may just have to accept things as they are and move on. Keep reminding yourself that you have a good thing going with a team-based approach and that it is well worth finding solutions for any disagreements.

Personal Crises

Try to remember that it is stressful to concentrate on your job responsibilities when a crisis is occurring in your personal life. Even if you cannot be working at your best, you do need to maintain effectiveness. In such cases, find support away from work, either with a good friend or with someone who has been through a similar crisis. Talk to this person about your feelings and the ways to cope with what is going on in your life.

You must take time for yourself, even if you need to schedule it. It does not matter what you find relaxing or invigorating, as long as it is something different from what you normally spend your time doing. Your mind and body both need diversion from work. If you prefer to spend this precious time alone, by all means do so; however, you should also find something that you enjoy doing in the company of others, if only for the social interaction. It is helpful to spend time with people who are not in education. It assists you in keeping a perspective on the world and in reminding you that your institution is not the center of the universe.

You also need to take time for some basic, down-to-earth fun, both by yourself and with your teammates. Such activities help to relieve the tension that builds when working in a team, and they also lead to creative ideas for solving problems. Try viewing a film clip together or reading a story and then discussing it. Questions such as "How does this relate to the problem we are trying to solve?" can be productive by focusing on something seemingly unrelated to the central issue to gain a fresh perspective. In addition, reading an article or a novel, going to a play, or attending a football game can be the catalyst to creative problem solving.

LAST WORDS

Above all, remember that you have been part of a major positive change in yourself and in your school. Teaming is hard work, but the rewards are many and well worth the time, effort, and professional integrity that you put into it.

As a final checklist, see if you have accomplished most of the following, and, if you have, you have indeed succeeded as a team:

- You have learned to trust the process of building a team. You have learned how to implement change, understanding that there is no rushing into things and that sustainable change is an evolving process in which all team members must be a part.
- You have learned that time is the most important element in a successful sustained process of team-based professional development.
- You have learned that money is important in that it can buy time for you to plan and work together.
- You have learned the importance of planning, particularly in using an action plan so that everyone knows who is doing what and when.
- You have learned that administrative support is basic to the success of your effort.
- You have learned that assessment is difficult and sometimes elusive but necessary to measure progress.
- You have learned the importance of communicating to the students, administration, parents, the school board, the general public, your peers, and—most of all—your teammates.
- You have learned the importance of documentation, not only for your own record keeping, but also for reports to the board and for verification to parents and others.
- You have learned to respect and accept that not everyone in your building or in your district holds the same beliefs that you do.
- You have learned that individuals in a team rise to expectations set for them.
- You have learned the necessity of reflection, and you have learned that, before the teaming process began, most of you had rarely taken the time to reflect, believing that it was a luxury you could not afford.
- You have learned that you have to trust your teammates and that they have to trust you.

- You have learned humility, that you did not always have all the answers.
- You have learned to use and acknowledge the creativity within yourself.
- You have learned the power of empowerment.
- You have learned the significance of small celebrations—that they are not luxuries but a special way of reflecting, commemorating, and planning.
- You have learned the absolute necessity and beauty of teamwork—and what that really means.
- Most of all, you have learned about yourself—that you can do anything that you set out to do and that you and your teammates are indeed a team.

References

Academic Innovations. (n.d.). *"Living proof": Tech prep in Delaware*. Retrieved March 4, 2006, from www.academicinnovations.com/int17.html

Bos, C. S., Mather, N., Narr, R. F., & Babur, N. (1999). Interactive, collaborative professional development in early literacy instruction: Supporting the balancing act. *Learning Disabilities Research and Practice, 14*(4), 227–238.

Boyer, E. L. (1983). *High school: A report on secondary education in America*. New York: Harper and Row.

Bredeson, P. (1992). *Responses to restructuring and empowerment initiatives: A study of teachers' and principals' perceptions of organizational leadership, decision making, and climate*. Paper presented at the annual meeting of the American Educational Research Association, San Fransicso.

Brockett, R. G., & Hiemstra, R. (1991). *Self-direction in adult learning: Perspectives on theory, research, and practice*. New York: Routledge.

Brookfield, S. (1993). Self-directed learning, political clarity, and the critical practice of adult education. *Adult Education Quarterly, 43*(4), 227–242.

Bruckerhoff, C., & Bruckerhoff, T. (1997). *EDUC 526 Experiential Science Learning I: A collaborative model for professional development, 1997 summative evaluation*. (ERIC Document Reproduction Service No. ED417958)

Calderon, M. (1995). *Dual language programs and team-teachers' professional development* (Report No. FL 023 591). Baltimore, MD: Center for Research on the Education of Students Placed at Risk. (ERIC Document Reproduction Service No. ED394274)

Clark, C. M. (1995). *Thoughtful teaching*. New York: Columbia University Press.

Clark, M. C. (1993). Transformational learning. In S. B. Merriam (Ed.), *An update on adult learning theory* (pp. 25–37). San Francisco: Jossey-Bass.

Cleland, J. V., Wetzel, K. A., Zambo, R., Buss, R. R., & Rillero, P. (1999). Science integrated with mathematics using language arts and technology: A model for collaborative professional development. *Journal of Computers in Mathematics and Science Teaching, 18*(2), 157–172.

Cranton, P., & King, K. P. (2003). Transformative learning as a professional development goal. *New Directions for Adult and Continuing Education, 98,* 31–37.

Darling-Hammond, L. (1996). The quiet revolution: Rethinking teacher development. *Educational Leadership, 53*(6), 4–10.

Elmore, R. F., & Burney, D. (1997, October). *School variation and systemic instructional improvement in Community School District #2, New York City* (High Performance Learning Communities Project RC-96-137002). Pittsburgh, PA: Learning Research and Development Center.

French, W. L., & Bell, C. H. (1995). *Organization development: Behavioral science interventions for organization improvement* (5th ed.). Englewood Cliffs, NJ: Prentice-Hall.

Fullan, M. (1991). *The new meaning of educational change.* New York: Teachers College Press.

Fullan, M. (2001). *Leading in a culture of change.* San Francisco: Jossey-Bass.

Fuller, F. F. (1969). Concerns of teachers: A developmental conceptualization. *American Educational Research Journal, 6*(2), 207–226.

Garet, M., Porter, A., Desimone, L., Birman, B., & Yoon, K. (2001, Winter). What makes professional development effective? Results from a national sample of teachers. *American Educational Research Journal, 38*(4), 915–945.

Glatthorn, A. A. (1990). Cooperative professional development: A tested approach, not a panacea. *Remedial and Special Education, 11*(4), 62.

Grow, G. (1991). Teaching learners to be self-directed: A stage approach. *Adult Education Quarterly, 41*(3), 125–149.

Guskey, T. R. (1986). Staff development and the process of teacher change. *Educational Researcher, 15*(5), 5–12.

Guskey, T. R. (1996, October 23). To transmit or to "construct"? *Education Week on the Web.* Retrieved from www.edweek.org

Guskey, T. R. (1997). *Evaluating professional development.* Thousand Oaks, CA: Corwin Press.

Haggstrom, G. W., Darling-Hammond, L., & Grissmer, D. W. (1988). *Assessing teacher supply and demand.* Santa Monica, CA: California Rand.

Hall, G. E., George, A., & Rutherford, W. L. (1979). *Measuring stages of concern about innovation: A manual for use of the SoC Questionnaire* (Report 3032). Austin: The University of Texas at Austin, Research and Development Center for Teacher Education. (ERIC Document Reproduction Service No. ED 147 342)

Hall, G. E., & Hord, S. M. (1987). *Change in schools: Facilitating the process.* Albany: State University of New York Press.

Hall, G. E., & Hord, S. M. (2006). *Implementing change: Patterns, principles, and potholes* (2nd ed.). Boston: Allyn and Bacon.

Hare, D., & Heap, J. (2001a). *Effective teacher recruitment and retention strategies in the Midwest: Who is making use of them?* Oak Book, IL: North Central Regional Educational Laboratory.

Hare, D., & Heap, J. (with Raack, L.). (2001b, June). Teachers recruitment and retention strategies in the Midwest: Where are they and do they work? *NCREL Policy Issues.* Retrieved July 27, 2006, from www.ncrel.org/policy/pubs/pdfs/pivol8.pdf

Haslam, M. B., & Seremet, C. P. (2001). *Strategies for improving professional development: A guide for school districts.* Alexandria, VA: New American Schools.

Horsley, D. L., & Loucks-Horsley, S. (1998). CBAM brings order to the tornado of change. *Journal of Staff Development, 19*(4), 17–20.

Hudis, P. A., Calderon, S., & Sanborn, J. (2005). *Research on professional development and the scholastic red model.* Berkeley, CA: MPR. Retrieved March 14, 2006, from teacher.scholastic.com/products/research/pdfs/RF_Scholastic Red_Model.pdf

Kelly, J. M. (1999, Summer). Free to teach, free to learn: A model of collaborative professional development that empowers teachers to reach diverse student populations. *Journal of Negro Education, 68*(3), 426–432.

Killion, J. (2002). *What works in the high school: Results-based staff development.* Oxford, OH: National Staff Development Council.

King, K. P. (2002). Educational technology professional development as transformative learning opportunities. *Computers & Education, 39,* 283–297.

Knowles, M. S. (1968). Andragogy, not pedagogy. *Adult Leadership, 16*(10), 351.

Knowles, M. S. (1984). *Andragogy in action.* San Francisco: Jossey-Bass.

Lawler, P. A., & King, K. P. (2003). Changes, challenges, and the future. *New Directions for Adult and Continuing Education, 98,* 83–91.

Lee, V. E., Smith, J. B., & Croninger, R. G. (1995, Fall). Another look at high school restructuring. *Issues in Restructuring Schools, 9,* 1–10.

Maslow, A. H. (1970). *Motivation and personality* (2nd ed.). New York: Harper-Collins.

McCaffrey, D., Hamilton, L., Stecher, B., Klein, S., Bulgari, D., & Robyn, A. (2001, November). Interactions among practices: Curriculum and achievement. The case of standards-based high school mathematics. *Journal for Research in Mathematics Education, 32*(5), 493–517.

McLaughlin, M., & Talbert, J. E. (1993). *Contexts that matter for teaching and learning: Strategic opportunities for meeting the nation's educational goals.* Stanford, CA: Stanford University. (ERIC Document Reproduction Service No. ED357023)

McLaughlin, M., & Talbert, J. E. (2001). *Professional communities and the work of high-school teaching.* Chicago: University of Chicago Press.

Melnick, S. A., & Schubert, M. B. (1997, March). *Curriculum integration: Essential elements for success.* Paper presented at the annual meeting of the American Educational Research Association, Chicago. (ERIC Document Reproduction Service No. ED414330)

Melnick, S. A., & Witmer, J. T. (1999, April). *Team-based professional development: A new model for professional growth.* Paper presented at the annual meeting of the American Educational Research Association, Montreal, Québec, Canada.

Merriam, S. B. (2001). Andragogy and self-directed learning: Pillars of adult learning theory. In S. B. Merriam (Ed.), *New directions for adult and continuing education* (pp. 3–13). San Francisco: Jossey-Bass.

Merriam, S. B., & Caffarella, R. S. (1999). *Learning in adulthood.* San Francisco: Jossey-Bass.

Mezirow, J. (1978). *Education for perspective transformation: Women's re-entry programs in community colleges.* New York: Columbia University, Teachers College.

Mezirow, J. (1985). A critical theory of self-directed learning. In S. Brookfield (Ed.), *Self-directed learning: From theory to practice* (pp. 17–30). San Francisco: Jossey-Bass.

National Staff Development Council. (2001). *About the standards.* Retrieved July 29, 2006, from www.nsdc.org/standards/about/index.cfm

Newmann, F., King, B., & Youngs, P. (2000, April). *Professional development that addresses school capacity.* Paper presented at the annual meeting of the American Educational Research Association, New Orleans, LA.

Newmann, F. M., & Wehlage, G. G. (1995). *Successful school restructuring: A report to the public and educators by the Center on Organization and Restructuring of Schools.* Madison, WI: University of Wisconsin, Center on Organization and Restructuring of Schools.

Osborne, B. (1993a). *Understanding change in a time of change.* (ERIC Document Reproduction Service No. ED358544)

Osborne, B. (1993b, March). *What education leaders need to know generally about quality and standards.* Paper presented at the Annual Conference on Creating the Quality School, Oklahoma City, OK. (ERIC Document Reproduction Service No. ED358543)

Page, J. (1994, April). *The teacher's role in restructuring: The power of one (a case study).* Paper presented at the annual meeting of the American Educational Research Association, New Orleans, LA.

Patterson, J. (1993). *Leadership for tomorrow's schools.* Alexandria, VA: Association for Supervision and Curriculum Development.

Peters, T., Schubeck, K., & Hopkins, K. (1995). A thematic approach: Theory and practice at the Aleknagik School. *Phi Delta Kappan, 76*(8), 633–636.

Renyi, J. (1996). *Teachers take charge of their learning: Transforming professional development for student success.* Washington DC: National Foundation for the Improvement for Education.

Rogers, C. R. (1969). *Freedom to learn.* Columbus, OH: Charles E. Merrill.

Rogers, C. R. (1983). *Freedom to learn for the 80s.* Columbus, OH: Charles E. Merrill.

Rosenholtz, S. J. (1989). Workplace conditions that affect teacher quality and commitment: Implications for teacher induction programs. *Elementary School Journal, 89*(4), 421–439.

Shroyer, M. G., Ramey-Gassert, L., Hancock, M., Moore, P., & Walker, M. (1995). Math, science, technology after school clubs and summer magnet school: Collaborative professional development opportunities for science educators. *Journal of Science Teacher Education, 6*(2), 112–119.

Shulman, L. S. (1986). Those who understand: Knowledge growth in teaching. *Educational Researcher, 15*(2), 4–14.

Siens, C. M., & Ebmeier, H. H. (1996). Developmental supervision and the reflective thinking of teachers. *Journal of Curriculum and Supervision, 11*(4), 299.

Sykes, G. (1996). Reform of and as professional development. *Phi Delta Kappan, 77*(7), 464–467.

Taylor, E. W. (1997). Building upon the theoretical debate: A critical review of the empirical studies of Mezirow's transformative learning theory. *Adult Education Quarterly, 48*(1), 34–59.

Tuckman, B. W. (1965). Developmental sequence in small groups. *Psychological Bulletin, 63,* 384–399.

U.S. Department of Education, Professional Development Team. (1995). *Mission and principles of professional development.* Washington, DC: Author.

Voltz, D. L. (1995). Peer coaching: A tool for collaborative professional development. *LD Forum, 20*(2), 28–30.

Wenglinsky, H. (2000, October). *How teaching matters: Bringing the classroom back into discussions of teacher quality.* Princeton, NJ: Milken Family Foundation and Educational Testing Service.

Wepner, S. B. (1993a). Technology and author studies. *Reading Teacher, 46*(7), 616–619.

Wepner, S. B. (1993b). Technology and thematic units: An elementary example on Japan. *Reading Teacher, 46*(5), 442–445.

WestEd. (2000). *Teachers who learn, kids who achieve: A look at schools with model professional development.* San Francisco: Author.

Williams, J., & Reynolds, T. D. (1993). Courting controversy: How to build interdisciplinary units. *Educational Leadership, 50*(7), 13–15.

Willis, S. (2002, March). Creating a knowledge base for teaching: A conversation with James Stigler. *Educational Leadership, 59*(6), 6–11.

Witmer, J. T. (2006). *Moving up!: A guidebook for women in educational administration* (2nd ed.). Lanham, MD: Rowman & Littlefield Education.

Witmer, J. T., & Melnick, S. A. (1997). *The Keystone Integrated Framework Project: A case study in curriculum integration.* Alexandria, VA: Association for Supervision and Curriculum Development.

Wong, H., & Wong, R. (2003, February). Effective teaching: How to retain new teachers. *Teachers.Net Gazette, 4*(2). Retrieved July 27, 2006, from teachers.net/gazette/FEB03/wong.html